CREATE YOUR OWN
STAGE LIGHTING

CREATE YOUR OWN
STAGE LIGHTING

Tim Streader and John A Williams

A SPECTRUM BOOK

Prentice-Hall, Inc., Englewood Cliffs, New Jersey 07632

Library of Congress Cataloging in Publication Data

Streader, Timothy
Create your own stage lighting

"A Spectrum Book"
Includes index
1. Stage lighting. I. Williams, John (John A.)
II. Title.
PN2091.E4S84 1985   792'.025   85-16728
ISBN O-13-189184-7
ISBN O-13-189176-6 (pbk.)

This book is available at a special discount when ordered in bulk quantities
Contact Prentice-Hall, Inc., General Publishing Division,
Special Sales, Englewood Cliffs, N.J. 07632.

First published by Prentice-Hall, Inc., in the USA 1985

10 9 8 7 6 5 4 3 2 1

Prentice-Hall International,Inc., *London*
Prentice-Hall of Australia Pty. Limited, *Sydney*
Prentice-Hall Canada Inc., *Toronto*
Prentice-Hall Hispanoamericana, S.A., *Mexico*
Prentice-Hall of India Private Limited, *New Delhi*
Prentice-Hall of Japan, Inc., *Tokyo*
Prentice-Hall of Southeast Asia Pte.Ltd., *Singapore*
Whitehall Books Limited, *Wellington, New Zealand*
Editoria Prentice-Hall do Brasil Ltda., *Rio de Janeiro*

ISBN 0-13-189184-7

ISBN 0-13-189176-6 {PBK.}

While every care has been taken to verify facts and methods
described in this book, neither the publishers nor the authors can
accept liability for any loss or damage howsoever caused. Legal
and safety requirements are subject to change and may vary with
the locality. It is the responsibility of the reader to verify current
regulations.

Typesetting by
Optic, London

Reproduction by
Redsend Limited, Birmingham

Printed in Great Britain by
Purnell & Sons (Book Production) Limited, Paulton

To Margarett Perryman
In memory of her encouragement to me
over the writing of this book (John A Williams)

Create Your Own Stage Lighting was conceived,
edited, and designed by
Thames Head Limited,
Avening, Tetbury,
Gloucestershire,
Great Britain

Editorial and Marketing director
Martin Marix Evans

Design and Production director
David Playne

Art editor
Barry Chadwick

Editor
Gill Davies

Consultant editor
Professor Robert A. Shakespeare,
Department of Theater and Drama,
Indiana University, Bloomington, Indiana, USA

Designers and illustrators
Heather Church
Terry Thomas
Jacquie Govier
Nick Allen
Tony De Saulles
Nick Hand
David Ganderton
Rob Wood

Other books in this series:

Create Your Own Stage Props
by Jacqui Govier
Create Your Own Stage Sets
by Terry Thomas
Create Your Own Stage Faces
by Douglas Young

Contents

10 History of stage lighting

The sixteenth century
The seventeenth century
The eighteenth century
The nineteenth century
The twentieth century

20 The role of a lighting designer

The creative role
Natural light
The organizing role

26 Equipment and basic techniques

Luminaires
The profile spot
The Fresnel spot
The pebble-convex luminaire
The Par
The flood
Luminaire maintenance
Lamps
Dimmers
Manual preset lighting boards
Manual cue sheet
Computer memory lighting control
Patching
Basic techniques
Lighting "structures"
Front light
Side light
Back light
Top or down light
Bottom or up light
Silhouette

52 Small beginnings

How to begin
Avoiding accidents
Using the luminaires
Color and special effects
Problems and afterthoughts

62 Lighting the stage

Pre-planning
The early stages
Script analysis and cue sheet
The discussion stage
Solving lighting problems

Awkward areas
Open rigs
Side light
Ceilings
Cycloramas
The model of the set
The lighting plan
Using symbols
The lighting design
The first rehearsal
Planning the rig
Choosing the lighting structure
Labeling the acting area
Lighting the stage sections
Key and fill light
Specials
Final decisions
The thrust stage
Lighting in the round (arena stage)

90 Production procedure

Pre-planning
The electrical team
The fit-up
Safety and rigging
Focusing
The focusing team
Rehearsals
The lighting rehearsal
The technical rehearsal
The dress rehearsal

100 Color

Using color carefully
Color theory
Primary colors
Color mixing
Lighting the acting area
Color practice
Color correction
Making a composite color
Color wheel
Choosing color
Color in action
Ring Round the Moon
Kipling
When the Wind Blows
Peter Pan
The Bengal Lancer
The Gondoliers

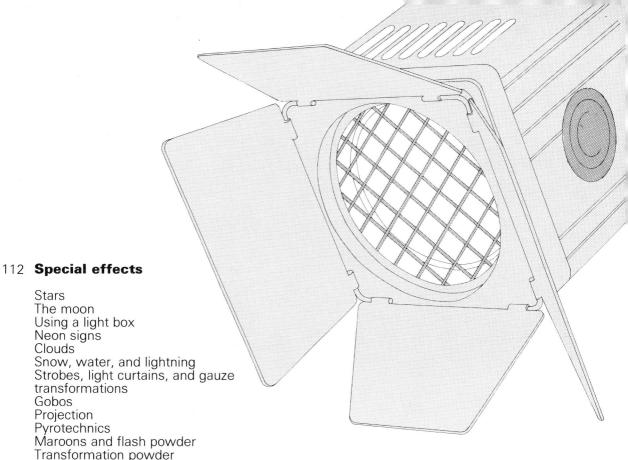

112 Special effects

Stars
The moon
Using a light box
Neon signs
Clouds
Snow, water, and lightning
Strobes, light curtains, and gauze
transformations
Gobos
Projection
Pyrotechnics
Maroons and flash powder
Transformation powder
Dry ice and smoke
Flickering fires
Oil lamps
Candles
Notes on projection

142 Lighting the stage with limited resources

Contol and color
Control boards
Warm and cool washes
Color wheel
Using available resources
"Dead areas"
Dimmers
Pairing lamps
Cross-plugging
Home-made lamps

150 Basic electrical theory and safety

Electricity
Making, using, and controlling
electrical energy
Alternating current
Fuses

Earthing (ground)
Safety
Cables
Circuit breakers
Calculating current
Series and parallel wiring
Transformers
Precautions

158 Lighting productions by John A. Williams

A Midsummer Night's Dream
The Recruiting Officer
When the Wind Blows
Oh What a Lovely War!
Lighting a musical
Lighting plans

186 Glossary

189 Index

192 Bibliography

192 Acknowledgments

Introduction

In the moments before a play begins, the auditorium is all bustle. Late arrivals apologize as they squeeze their way through to their seats, sweet papers rustle, programs are passed along the row, and general gossip is exchanged. The audience is divided into many separate little groups. Then, suddenly, the lights dim and the last snatches of conversation hush away as the audience becomes as one. The world of make-believe is about to begin, heralded by a change of lighting state.

This is a convention readily accepted. It may, on occasions, be augmented by an orchestral introduction to the evening's entertainment, but it is really this initial darkening of the auditorium that signals to the audience that now they must prepare themselves to become a part of what is to follow. As the lights are then raised on the curtain or stage, all attention is drawn in that direction.

Thus the lighting demonstrates, at the beginning of every performance, that it is a very powerful tool.

Lighting can take many forms and guises. It may be stunning and dramatic, or subtly self-effacing, so that the audience react to its effects while scarcely realizing its presence. Its initial command of audience attention before the curtain is raised may perhaps be divorced from the content of the play itself but, during the rest of the production, the lighting should be an integral part of the drama.

Light can mold the space on the stage with all its architectural characteristics, its color, and its own very elemental dramatic qualities. It is, after all, a form of energy, a basic requirement: light and dark, day and night, black and white — a world of contrasts. Paint the stage with these effectively and the audience will be better able to relate to all the other aspects of production. Moreover, and most important of all, light enables the actor to be seen.

All this can be achieved by technological expertise. It will be necessary to analyze the job in hand, sort out the necessary tools, and then set to work to implement them properly. However, the manipulation of light to create a visual concept is not purely a technical task. It is very much an artistic one and this book sets out to explore both aspects of lighting the stage — the mechanics and the design.

All the basic equipment and the instruments of light are discussed. These include lamps and luminaires, as well as dimmers, control boards, and computer systems. The means to exploit this equipment to the full, by understanding just how a luminaire's position and angle will alter its effect, is also explained; and the electrical principles involved, special effects, and the use of color.

This technical know-how is supplemented by an analysis of production procedure so it can be seen how the lighting plan for any show can be undertaken in a logical and practical fashion, from the first evaluation of the script, through discussion and practical planning, to the final dress rehearsal.

There is much to learn. A brief history of early stage lighting explores the changing fashions in lighting, reflecting both the scientific developments in the world around and the way attitudes to theater and light evolved over the years.

The role of the lighting designer can never be divorced from the technicalities of the medium but neither should it ever be totally contained within them. It is a creative art form, and, as such, is a very satisfying element of stage production in which to be involved.

Ideal conditions rarely prevail. This book is not purely for the theorists and so takes into account the fact that resources may be limited and the budget already overstretched. How to cope with limited equipment is fully discussed in one chapter, *Lighting the stage with limited resources,* and is borne in mind throughout the book. Moreover, the fact that anyone new to the field may find it difficult to relate to the subject initially is alleviated by the inclusion of the *Small beginnings* chapter and a comprehensive glossary.

A check should always be made on local regulations and legal requirements so that suitable precautions can be taken and the production will not be marred by any accident or last-minute panic to fulfil safety requirements.

Safety is a major consideration. Hazard symbols may be found throughout the book and these indicate where the procedure may be potentially dangerous and caution is required. A chapter on basic electrical theory and safety serves to explain in simple terms, the principles which are involved when lighting the stage — but is only a brief synopsis of these. For this reason, anyone who is to undertake the handling of electrical equipment will need a far deeper grasp of the subject than this chapter can supply. It is to be hoped, therefore, that much wider reading will precede practical application of the theories that are discussed. Several books on the subject have been included in the Bibliography.

The book recognizes that there can never be a substitute for real experience, dealing with the particular problems of each production, working through the planning stage, setting up the rig, and the rehearsals — until the moment comes when the lighting is being used in live theater. Only then can the results be properly seen and evaluated. However, it is possible through the chapter on John A. Williams' own lighting productions, to share a little of his experience as a lighting designer. We can see lighting in action, in the real world rather than the pages of a book, as many of the theories are put into practice, in live situations in the theater.

It is hoped the book will be invaluable in discovering how to use a wide range of theater lighting and effects, even for the beginner. At the same time, the professional standards of the authors have been in no way compromised through their exploration of the subject as it might be applied to amateur or student theater, as well as the professional stage.

Many visual elements combine on the stage to create space and time and highlight the action. Lighting is undoubtedly the most mobile of these. Used skilfully, it will focus attention, as required, throughout the production.

Then, as the curtains close on the final applause, it will be the raising of the house lights that seems to "release" the captive audience, allowing them once again to become individuals as the auditorium fills with light.

◇ Watch out for these hazard symbols throughout the book. They will identify any potentially dangerous situations!

History of stage lighting

Modern stage lighting has changed dramatically in recent years, with computer control, memory systems, and all that technology has to offer; so much so that the lighting of the previous decade might well seem historical by comparison! It is almost impossible for us to visualize lighting by gaslight or candles a century ago.

There is, however, a great deal to be learned by looking back into the past. An appreciation of how lighting developed will help to underline the principles involved. Understanding how a particular play might have looked when lit by the methods then prevailing could perhaps make for a more sympathetic approach when lighting it today.

It might even be possible to replicate some of the effects.

If nothing else, realizing the problems of the past ought to make us appreciate all the possibilities of today; and the inventiveness and ingenuity of early artists in this field should be an inspiration to every lighting designer!

The earliest forms of theater took place out of doors with the open sky above as the source of light with all its natural random changes of mood and intensity. Presumably the position and design of the structure (when there was one) and the time of day had some bearing on how the light fell, whether shadows were cast, and so on.

Perhaps torches might have been used for dramatic effect at night. Normally, however, the audience and actors alike would have shared the same sky and weather. There would have been no separation of actors and audience by light and dark and no dimming of lights to announce the start of the performance, conventions we nowadays take for granted.

A visit to an open-air performance today may be reminiscent of the past but is probably regarded as a unique experience, set apart from traditional theater.

So how did it all begin? What records remain of the various steps along the way?

11

The sixteenth century

Stage lighting evolved, as did many technological and artistic advances, with experiments and specialized branches of exploration, some of which can be seen in retrospect as "dead-ends". It grew with the scientific knowledge which fed it, but as it is also an art form, it reflected as well the particular personalities spearheading its evolution.

The history of stage lighting as we know it begins at about this time, when theater had moved indoors and at last some control could be exercised over lighting levels and their effect on the production.

The Italian influence

Leone di Soni, an Italian, stated that a tragedy was best performed in a lower light level than that required by a comedy. Thus the lighting was now obviously being seen as a reflection of the mood of the play being enacted.

At this time, Angelo Ingegneri also suggested that the stage appeared much brighter when contrasted with a darkened auditorium, a fact still exploited today, especially if the available lighting is limited.

In 1539, San Gallo of Florence imitated the sun by filling a crystal sphere with water and lighting it from behind with candles. This sun "rose" at the beginning of the play, moved across the "sky" and then "set" as the action closed.

Moons were represented in a similar way, while lightning consisted of pieces of jagged-shaped wood covered in tinsel and flown across on wires!

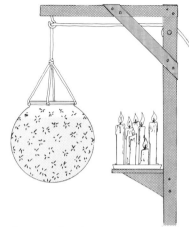

A crystal sphere

Liquid tinting existed at this time but was found to reduce the light's intensity so it was conserved for such special effects as jeweled windows and festive lights on buildings. Thus the lighting designer's golden rule held true even then: The main function of the lighting was to illuminate the actor. In fact the Renaissance artists at this time began to formulate many of the artistic principles which are still valid today.

Lighting and scenic effects

In 1545, yet another Italian, Sebastiano Serlio, developed the use of lighting with scenery. The actual lighting emanated from a single chandelier, centrally positioned, but his scenic views were designed and painted to look as though they were lit from one side only.

Roundels and windows were made of transparent materials with lights placed behind. Glass containers which held colored water, or sometimes even wine, were fastened on to battens and used to reflect different tints. Stage thunder and lightning was effectively created and "heavenly bodies" flew through the air by the means of wire and thread!

In 1585, Scamozzi placed lights at the side of his scenery, which was found to be far more effective than existing forms of lighting. This idea was taken up by Inigo Jones, who introduced it into the English theater.

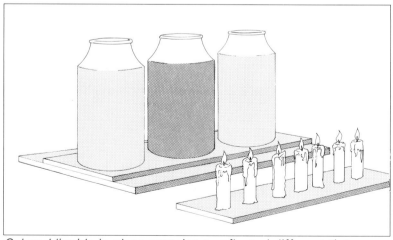

Colored liquids in glass containers reflected different tints

The seventeenth century

In 1665, Sabbattini developed the concept of lighting from the side. He demonstrated that lighting from one side had a far more pleasing effect that when the stage was lit from the front.

In fact, the Renaissance artists developed and mastered most of the lighting techniques which continued to be used until the late eighteenth century.

The masque

It was now that the masque became fashionable, with great expense lavished on effects which became ever more extravagant and spectacular. Through this medium, the first really unified "scenographic" picture appeared on the English stage in *The Masque of Blackness* when motion, light, and costume all contributed to the dramatic effect.

A single stage set incorporated a moving sea with breaking waves created by perspective illusion. No less than twelve separate masques appeared on this ocean, set in a huge shell and accompanied by moving sea-horses, mermaids, and sea monsters. These were all illumined by a chevron of lights which also rocked on the ocean waves, while twelve torch bearers directed extra light on to the rich silk of the costumes.

Set above this heaving ocean was a cloudy night sky, from which a personified moon was later to appear, dressed in white and silver, sitting on a throne, and crowned with a sphere of light which was to illumine all the clouds. The heavens were vaulted with blue silk and studded with silver stars.

This, no doubt, all seems too rich to our modern taste, going "over the top" with a vengeance! However, it must certainly have made quite an impression on the audience at the time, and was an explosion of new ideas, a journey of discovery into all that could be theatrically achieved.

Oil lamps and candlelight

It comes as quite a shock to realize that all these lighting effects discussed so far were being achieved by candle power and oil lamps. Candles were prefered in the auditorium as oil lamps produced too much smoke and smell, and even these needed trimming every twenty minutes or so.

There was usually only one chandelier placed over the forestage to light both this and the auditorium. Down-stage lighting was provided by footlights, which were mounted behind a parapet set a short distance in front of the stage. Perhaps the mystical effect of some of the scenes was helped by the misty haze of smoke all these lights produced!

On the stage the lights were concealed from view (masked). Behind the proscenium and the wings were placed vertical poles supporting several oil lamps set in evenly spaced rings (the forerunner of modern "lighting trees" or "booms"!)

Other lamps were mounted on horizontal battens at the back of the front valance and the borders. Tinsel, mica, and even polished copper basins were used to make reflectors to increase the efficiency of these early lamps.

The seventeenth century

Darkening the stage

Next time you watch the lights slowly fade out on a scene, imagine how difficult it must have been in the past to darken the stage. There were three possible methods:

First, the lights were simply extinguished. This could be very inconvenient if the stage needed to appear brightly lit again, a few moments later.

A better method was to suspend open cylinders over the candles. These cylinders could then be raised or lowered as necessary.

Third, the lamps could be mounted on rotating poles which were able to swivel away from or toward the area of stage concerned.

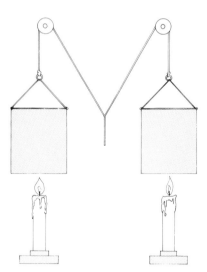

Lighting takes many forms

When an exceptionally bright light was required, these were often concealed in a specially designed scenic device. Yet another grotto, shell, or cloud would be placed conveniently near the object or performer who was to benefit from the extra light. These trappings all incorporated a downstage rim to hide the lamps.

Footlights were now being used in England, largely because of the necessity to fully appreciate the dancers' legs! Fire was also a major problem, with all these open flames exposed. Oil wicks were often floated on water or oil vats to alleviate the risk — hence the term "floats".

The year 1610 saw one of the first performances enacted at night. Hitherto any productions that continued into the late afternoon merely used the light still available through the windows and a chandelier or two. It is worth noting that this is another convention we may take for granted. Theater has only comparatively recently been a creature of the night!

Most performances had to be daytime activities because of the lighting difficulties. The length of time available for a performance was not restricted to the shorter evening period and many lasted for five or six hours or more, with lunch being consumed during the course of the play. This is why so many old plays require drastic cutting to fit into today's evening niche.

Samuel Pepys attended some evening performances and he noted in his diary that the actresses made quite a show by candlelight! He also commented, with considerably less enthusiasm, that the candlelight caused headaches!

Lighting was also used at this time as a diversion from scene changing in the interval. At Tethys Festival, music was used to smother the noise of the machinery involved when the audience was entertained, in between the scene changes, by three revolving circles of light and glass descending before their eyes.

By 1640 masques were becoming less popular. The exploration of motion and light had reached its zenith in the myriad candles and colored lamps, the exotic scenery, and baroque costumes.

England was being compared unfavorably with France and Italy for not yet knowing how to position lights to their best advantage. There were many quarrels over the complex, and very cumbersome machinery required for these spectacular productions, so much so that one producer reverted to a simplistic production, using just one light center stage.

In 1674 a production of *The Tempest* at the Dorset Garden Theater used, for the first time, the dimming of lights. As the ship sank all the house lights were slowly dimmed and a shower of fire fell. This was achieved by raising the chandelier and lowering the footlights, while shields were dropped over the wing lights.

In general, the auditorium still remained lit. The glorious pomp of the masque was still sometimes reflected in the grand finale of a play, with transparent silk backcloths lit from behind to reveal scenes of heaven and deities.

The eighteenth century

During this period light gradually became far more controlled. The lights placed on vertical ladders behind the wings were able to be dimmed by "scene blinds" and footlights were mounted on pivots so they too could be more easily lowered when dimming.

Henry Angelo

Henry Angelo visualized his scenes as transparencies. He advocated far greater subtlety in scenic design, and to help achieve this, he introduced transparent backcloths behind which visionary figures could be glimpsed. Color was more carefully controlled too by means of silk screens of scarlet, crimson, and blue. By placing a powerful light in front of these and then turning them towards the scenes, their colors could be reflected in turn so that the stage appeared to be on fire.

David Garrick

By 1765 David Garrick reputedly introduced many new lighting techniques, though it is unclear today which reforms can actually be credited to him. We do know that hoops of candles, indiscriminately hung over the stage so that they covered buildings and landscapes, were replaced after his tour abroad. Instead he installed a new type of batten incorporating lamps and reflectors which could be swivelled, so that different degrees of light could be obtained according to the time of day required.

Philip de Loutherbourg

French scene designer, Philip de Loutherbourg, was engaged by David Garrick in 1771. His improvements at Drury Lane introduced higher lighting costs. They rose from about £340 per annum to around £1970. His ideas were based on the Italian Renaissance and he favored wild landscapes, picturesque effects, and strong dramatic lighting. He also believed the English temperament "nurtured on mists and nuances of light" would appreciate the less formal and more romantic approach. He became a pioneer in this field and took complete control of the visual side of production in a way that had not occurred since Inigo Jones.

The theater's lighting system, scene shifting, costumes, scenery, machinery, and decor were all to contribute to this unified picture and had to be adapted accordingly.

The range of lighting effects was expanded and far more subtle transitions were made possible. The use of transparent colored silks to reflect light on to the scenes was developed so that a "vast body and brilliancy of colour" could be readily used "with enchanting effect". For instance, a forest scene could suddenly change from green to blood red (a transition which was pronounced "garish" by Gainsborough).

At last machinery miracles had disappeared. Truth to nature became the ultimate aim. Philip de Loutherbourg was described as "The first artist who showed that by a just disposition of light and shade....and perspective, the eye of the spectator might be so effectively deceived.... as to take the produce of art for real nature".

By 1781 oil lighting was improved by cylindrical wicks and glass chimneys which made the light steadier and much brighter. Moreover the chimneys could be colored, which simplified these effects. The improvements in lighting enabled actors to move further behind the proscenium arch.

Oil lamp with glass chimney

De Loutherbourg demonstrated the effects of this improved light in his model theater. The passing of opaque or colored materials in front of illuminated semi and fully transparent surfaces was greatly admired when it took the form of the sun and moon reflected on water. By 1785 De Loutherbourg, and some ballet companies, were exploring the use of gauzes.

Panoramas and dioramas

It was now that panoramas began to appear, first seen in Edinburgh and mostly used for pantomime, as were the first dioramas. This innovation consisted of partly transparent scenery, which remained stationary while screens and shutters manipulated natural light to give a variety of effects.

The nineteenth century

The arrival of gas lighting

The beginning of this century saw dramatic changes with the introduction of gas lighting. In 1822, the New Opera in Paris opened with all the latest developments, including gas lights and a water system to create waterfalls and fountains.

Gas light had in fact first been used on stage in Philadelphia in 1816 and it reached Covent Garden and Drury Lane a year later. There was as yet no gas-mains system, so each theater had to provide its own independent supply and its own maintenance.

Despite the oppressive heat and fumes the gas produced, its remarkable effects were soon fully appreciated. The sudden appearance of the lights from out of the gloom was seen as the striking of daylight, white, regular, and pervading. For the first time every part of the stage could be seen with equal clarity. Its greater flexibility and its intensity made possible many transitions, such as the sun setting, twilight pervading the sky, or a starlit night glimmering above the sea. Many new possibilities opened up, and the invention of mirror flats to reflect the light added to the range of effects.

By 1843 gas was installed at the Comedie-Française in Paris but the actresses complained that the new light was rather too harsh, so the footlights here remained as oil lamps. In some theaters, footlights developed into a large cluster, "the rose", to which actors had to move if making an important speech.

Limelight and the carbon arc

Limelight was used in Covent Garden in the 1830s to add to the brilliance of dioramas of Italian and Alpine scenery. However it was found to be rather expensive and was not used again until 1851.

By the 1840s, theaters in France were also experimenting with limelight, which had been invented in 1816 by Thomas Drummond, an Englishman. Two cylinders of compressed gas (one of hydrogen and one of oxygen) were directed against a column of lime, which was then heated to produce a great incandescence.

In 1846, a carbon arc (first demonstrated by Sir Humphry Davy in 1808) was used at the Opera to create a rising sun effect. It was rather a harsh, flickering light and somewhat noisy. The system was much improved in 1876 with the invention of the Jablochkov Candle by a young Russian engineer living in Paris.

New inventions and improvements

In England, gas was becoming ever more available and widely adopted. There was a new-found sense of freedom now that there were no wicks to trim or candles to replace. Gas lights could be better positioned and so border lights became more popular. The invention of the fishtail burner in 1850 lessened the fumes and made the system all the more efficient, as did the introduction of the "Gas-Table" (the equivalent of today's Gas Board).

At last the gradual dimming of house lights could be readily effected. By 1849 the curtain of darkness had dropped between the spectator and the stage.

The greater flexibility of lights helped the development of transformation scenes using painted gauzes. Scenes were apparently magically revealed and then rendered invisible once again.

Limelight was again introduced and its mellow, brilliant rays lent themselves to atmospheric scenes and moonlight, but it still required constant supervision.

All these new lighting systems made dramatic differences to stage lighting, both in Europe and America, but artistic principles were still sadly lacking. Moreover the lighting was as yet only general illumination, without any of the spotlights that are now so familiar to us. In 1860, however, a hood and lens was added to the carbon arc to create the very first spotlight.

During the 1860s, Charles Fechter, manager of the Lyceum, introduced an early prototype of the cyclorama. It was really an overhead sky-cloth which "mingled softly with the horizon". He also organized a system of gas footlights below the sloping level of the stage, so arranged that the whole float could be sunk and its red or green lights turned up instantaneously or gradually, as appropriate.

Sir Henry Irving

In 1878 Sir Henry Irving took over the management of the

The twentieth century

Lyceum. He was really the first British producer to make an art of stage lighting and to analyze and supervise its use in a detailed fashion.

His first innovation was to split up the footlights and borders into different sections with separate colors and controls. He also experimented with transparent lacquered glass, despite criticism that this made the lighting arbitrary and distracting. In order to prevent lighting spill, Irving introduced the use of black masking pieces at the front of the stage.

Thirty gas men were needed to mount and operate all the lights at the Lyceum as the auditorium was, for the first time, consistently darkened during the performance.

The arrival of electricity

The incandescent gas mantle had by now made the lighting even safer, but at the end of the century, electricity began to replace it. The potential of Edison's discoveries were immediately exploited by the theaters of the world. There were those, however, who prefered the richer, more atmospheric gaslight, including Sir Henry Irving.

In 1881 Richard D'Oyly Carte opened up his new theater in London, the Savoy, with Gilbert and Sullivan's *Patience*. This was the first time in London that a play was lit throughout with the new electricity.

Sir Hubert von Herkomer

At a little theater in Bushey, Herkomer was experimenting further with the use of gauze and backcloths. His cloud effects were so convincing that the audience had to be shown that this was only an illusion. He was one of the first to abolish footlights because their light was so unnatural, and to see the possibilities of projection, using a magic lantern to create his moving clouds.

Herkomer developed many of our modern principles. He showed that inexpensive materials, if properly lit, could be more effective than skilfully painted silks. He strove to achieve a total work of art, insisting that "it is through the management of light that we touch the real magic of art".

This was echoed in a production of *Faust* in 1886, when color and movement were harmonized, Mephistopheles' scarlet cloak echoing the sunset, and the lighting producing both warm sunshine and cooler brown and gray shades — a far more naturalistic approach.

By this time nearly all English theaters were using electric lighting, although the low wattage then provided meant that carbon arc and limelight were still quite important elements of the lighting, and remained so until after the First World War.

Before very long, significant improvements in the design of lamp filaments made higher wattages possible, and by 1913 1kw lamps were available in Europe. Spotlights were becoming far more popular, and those mounted in the auditorium gradually replaced the footlights. There was much experimentation at this time with new lighting positions and bridges and the use of color.

Adolphe Appia

Adolphe Appia, a Swiss-born German, was the man who probably had the greatest influence on stage lighting and scenic design at the turn of the century. Initially his ideas were denounced as impractical but in actual fact they had an enormous impact, both on practical applications of the new technology and on the whole approach to lighting.

He was one of the first designers to see the real possibilities of electric light, how it could be used to show the ever-changing quality of natural light, and its diffusion and movement. Up to this time, stage lighting had always been inexorably static.

He was also very interested in using 3-D to create far more realistic sets. He employed light to accentuate the solidity of structures by creating a strong contrast between the highlights and the shadows.

Appia had worked with Wagner and applied his precept of trying to establish a unity between all the various theater arts. He saw light as the most important element in fusing these creative forces. Appia dreamed of manipulating and orchestrating light, like a musical score!

Previously lighting had been simple, crude, and clumsy to operate, so it was usually only raised and lowered at the beginning and the end of a play. This was now all to change.

The twentieth century

The plasticity of light and its direction were to be controlled at last. Sets were more realistic and the lighting changes became unobtrusive; no longer dramatic transitions "before your very eyes".

Appia argued that the director should control all elements of production and that the lighting was primarily for the actor, not the scenery. (In the United States, the scenic designer was actually responsible for the lighting.) Appia's reforms led to mobile overhead illumination which could help mold the gestures of the actors and highlight the patterns and shapes of the groups on the stage. Light should not be squandered on the superficial.

With better color projection, painted colors became less important. The invention of an arc lamp which could be used for indirect illumination and diffusion helped in the realization of all these ideas, and Appia's theories spread throughout Europe.

Edward Gordon Craig

Edward Gordon Craig, who was an English contemporary of Appia's, was greatly influenced by him and especially admired his ideas on spatial abstraction. Craig was also regarded as an impractical theorist, especially as he took Appia's ideas one stage further and insisted on director control. He really would have liked to dispense with actors altogether and convey the action by scenery, dance, movement, and light. Perhaps even the play itself was superfluous! Everything could be reduced to its essential elements. He even suggested staging *Macbeth* in two colors only, brown for the man and gray for the mist.

Craig also further developed Herkomer's gauze device. He added lighting from above to give greater depth of color. Gelatines of blue, amber, and green lit a backcloth which was gray or ultramarine, depending on the mood of the opera. Then, in 1902, he replaced the painted backcloth with a simpler one which consisted of graduated colors, from white at the base to indigo at the top.

The German influence

At about the same time, German innovators were further developing the use of the cyclorama. Either a backing was stretched over vertical rollers or it was dome shaped to partially cover the stage and prevent awkward edges being visible. In England, Reinhardt adapted the flat version with curved ends and used it as a light reflector. Bands of colored silk travelled on rollers and reflected luminous soft tints on to the neutral cyclorama. This was a far more gentle and subtle affect than direct lighting on a painted backcloth.

During the 1920s there was something of a battle between the German lighting system of localized spotlighting and the compartment batten, made popular in Britain by Samoiloff. It provided mainly all-over floodlighting and color effects, and was also being used in the United States. In general, there were four main steps forward; the more efficient lamp, a better reflector, improvement in color techniques, and a shifting theater convention which began to emphasize selective control of the stage picture.

By now light was much brighter. With each new source of light, from candles and oil, through to gas and electricity, and then the more powerful reflector battens. The increase in light intensity was significant, even dramatic in some cases, but by today's standards, it would still seem comparatively dark!

In 1933 aluminum scenery, which would catch the light, was introduced by Theodore Komisarjevsky. His *King Lear* made a great impression. It was performed on a spacious, bare, stepped stage, the action taking place in pools of light which flowed, swirled, and changed in color.

Harold Ridge installed what was then one of the finest lighting systems in the world at the Cambridge Festival Theatre. He was a disciple of Appia and implemented many of his ideas. Settings and costumes were illuminated with moving symbolic color. Light was the predominant factor, used to suggest within the hollow box of the stage all the form, color, and symbolism that Appia had dreamed about.

Front projection was used most dramatically on the cyclorama in *The Hairy Ape*, when the struggle of the gorilla was projected in gigantic shadows, and in 1931 Harold Short's production of *Waltzes from Vienna* at the Alhambra used great batteries of spotlights to supplement the normal battens and footlights.

In the United States, the use of the profile spot dates from about this time, being introduced on a large scale. British lamp manufacturers were unable to make a suitable lamp for almost thirty years, and the difference in voltages prevented their importation.

Emphasis on the visual creation of light continued to occupy the lighting designer's imagination throughout the next twenty years or so. Not all of the experimentation was wholly practical. In some cases, the innovation shocked audiences. A production of *Tannhauser* in 1954, which used light and projection instead of scenery, caused quite an outrage.

In 1956 Brecht encouraged the use of projected photographs and moving pictures. The impact of slides and films could be quite stunning (as seen later in *Oh What a Lovely War!*). Brecht also advocated the use of stark white light.

During the post-war years, the American musical made an important impression on the world of theater. When *Oklahoma* was first produced, it unveiled a totally different experience in choreography and staging. This led to the continuing influence of "The Big Musical" with all its color and lavish production techniques.

Modern lighting equipment was now readily available, with most of the luminaires and dimmers familiar today. These have obviously been improved and refined. The age of the computer has accelerated this continuous pattern of finer technology and ease of control.

The creative element

It is still the ideas and the application of the lighting designer's vision that enables all these different pieces of equipment to be so effective.

Today designers, such as Ralph Koltai, are exploring the use of plastics because of the great light quality that these contain. His abstract designs have transferred to the stage the optical and illusory effects of modern art.

We have come a long way from crystal spheres lit by candles, and even further from the open sky. Lighting effects have swung from the ostentatious heavenly vistas used in the seventeenth century to the close imitation of nature, and then to symbolic pools of color. Sometimes a new invention has spearheaded new ideas, and sometimes the ideas have sought out the practical means to make them possible.

Just what the future holds cannot be predicted. The past can be seen as a carousel of many different techniques and fashions, but throughout it is the role of the lighting designer that has grown consistently. It is the way the available lighting has been exploited and its visual impact on the stage that has helped each era to achieve its own particular magic.

The role of a lighting designer

What is a lighting designer? Such a person did not exist in the days of Greek drama and does not exist today in open street theater. So what exactly happens when theater moves indoors? How does lighting contribute to a play, and what is the role of the lighting designer? It would be more accurate, in fact to ask, "What roles?" because there are many.

The lighting designer will soon find that the role extends far beyond simple illumination of the stage. He or she is a working member of a team, whose overall aim is to achieve a successful and co-ordinated theatrical production. So, when all is not well with other aspects of the production, the lighting designer may find himself coming to the rescue and trying to adapt the lighting to help a fellow member of the production team.

For instance, the designer may be asked, "Can you light out those wrinkles?" when a stage cloth has been badly hung or creased; or a set designer may say, "I haven't achieved quite the right color on that wall; can you light a little more blue into it?" Next might come the director's admission, "I have blocked that little scene rather badly over there; can you divert the emphasis to the group stage left?"

So what roles should the lighting designer expect to play?

The creative role

Design and illumination

First and foremost, a lighting designer should be an artist, not a lighting mechanic or someone who has just "come to do the lights". Most people with a fairly basic knowledge of stage lighting should be able to illuminate an acting area. To add a design quality to this basic lighting lifts that person into a different category. He or she becomes a lighting designer.

Lighting the actor

It is still true to say that the main function of the lighting designer, before attempting any special effects or innovations, is to light the stage so that the actor can be seen. It is totally useless to have a beautifully illuminated stage and set, if the acting area is so badly lit that the actors' faces are hidden in shadow.

So, first and foremost, do remember the golden rule: light the stage so that the actors can be seen.

It has been said that an actor who cannot be seen, cannot be heard. There is definitely a close relationship between the two senses. In any event, actors need to be audible and visible, and it is the lighting designer's first task to see to the latter requirement.

Lighting the stage

Having achieved this basic illumination of the actor, the designer should then light the stage in a way that will be creative, enhancing both the set and the costumes, as well as highlighting the drama. It should never, in any way, detract from these other aspects of the production. A good lighting designer will plan to add mood and atmosphere to the piece, but still keep all the above requirements in mind while doing so.

Special effects

The lighting designer is often called upon to create special effects. Depending on the organization of each individual theater, these effects may not be restricted to lighting effects. They may be any effect that is electrical — or powered by electrical means — such as smoke, dry-ice, pyrotechnics (bangs and flashes), and all the electrical props.

The production team

Throughout all this, the lighting designer should also be aware of the set designer's problems, particularly that of "masking" ; that is the way the set can both hide (and sometimes obstruct) all the mechanics of a play, including all the equipment the lighting necessarily requires.

Consultation with a lighting designer early in the planning stage could solve difficulties that might otherwise become major problems in the later development of the play.

It is obviously beneficial to both parties if the lighting designer can work closely with the set designer to achieve a mutually compatible visual concept.

This is particularly important when certain parts of a set require lighting to make them work — such as backlit cloths or gauze transformations.

The script

In these early stages, it is always a bonus if a lighting designer extracts information from the script, over and above the more obvious requirements dictated by the time of day or by the switching on and off of lights. There is often far more to be discovered on a closer investigation of the playscript. So it can be seen that a lighting designer can contribute a great deal to the conception of a production — even before seeing the set or costume designs. He or she should never be just a puppet who illuminates only other people's ideas. Otherwise the role will revert to that of an illuminator, as opposed to a lighting designer.

Awareness and observation

Like many other artists or designers, a lighting designer can, of course, borrow or develop further other people's ideas. Do not be too insular. Visits to libraries, art galleries, and so on (perhaps in order to research visual aids) can often spark off an idea. So, of course, can nature itself. The various qualities of simple daylight are a kaleidoscope of many different colors, changing moods and atmospheres. Nature achieves unwittingly all the lighting "structures" we shall study later, from side light at early morning sunrise, moving on through every angle up to top or back light at noon, and then returning to side light at dusk. In doing so, it can produce an array of vivid colors we would scarcely dare reproduce on stage but which are quite natural out of doors.

Natural light

Shadow cast by a tree when sun is overhead

Reflection of the sun on water

Pattern of shadows cast by a fence

Angled shadows as the sun moves round

The organizing role

Management and mechanics

Lighting designers will need to be competent managers; they must organize people and production scheduling, and allocate time accordingly.

When the designer is "on-site", the achievement of the final design in the time allowed is very much a team effort.

For instance, the lighting crew may well have worked all through the previous night — or even have spent several days constructing the lighting "rig". Now an arduous focusing session lies ahead of them.

At this point, the lighting designer arrives, probably feeling full of enthusiasm and certainly far more wide-awake than the crew. It is as well to remember the many hours of work already undertaken by the crew. Respect and appreciation of their efforts at this time will result in mutual co-operation. A jammed shutter might be released in seconds, or take many precious minutes to free if the crew is disgruntled!

Ideally, the lighting designer should be capable of estimating the time required for the crew to rig; and how much time he or she needs to focus and light.

Allow about three minutes to focus each luminaire. In actual fact, most of them will take less than two minutes, although sometimes the inaccessability of a luminaire may lengthen the focusing session.

Sometimes, for example, lamps over a set can be reached only by the painstaking manipulation of ladders or Tallescopes" (used when it is necessary to focus by estimation).

"Bouncing bars" (or light pipes) may have to be used. The lighting bar is lowered to a reachable position, the focus estimated, and the luminaire then returned to its "dead" (the final hanging position). This process may have to be repeated several times before the focus is correct.

Experience will give the lighting designer a better grasp of time estimation. Meanwhile, it is preferable to over-estimate. It is much better to have a pat on the back for finishing a couple of hours early than having to contend with bad feeling because the work takes two hours longer than scheduled.

Any stress or frustration will be most unwelcome at the next stage — the lighting session. This takes place at the end of the "fit-up", when the lights are rigged and focused and the set is up and working.

The last thing a lighting designer wants is pressure to finish during the lighting session as it is at this stage that the designer's final visual concept is realized.

Sometimes, however, the set may not be ready on time and this is often a frustrating delay for the lighting team.

Hopefully, all will be well. The set is up and functioning and the focusing is complete. The lighting crew have not turned hostile, and, despite all the pressures, team spirit prevails!

The lighting designer has succeeded in his role as a manager. Now it is possible to revert once more to the role of an artist, a creator of time, space, and atmosphere, all through the medium of light.

Aims

To be a designer, not just an illuminator

To light the stage so that the actors can be seen

To analyze the script carefully and fulfil all its dictates

To work well as a member of the production team and co-operate with the others at the planning stage, giving practical help to alleviate any later problems that arise

To enhance both the set and the costumes

To be creative, using light to fill the stage with mood and atmosphere

To be able to provide the appropriate special effects

To be a good manager of people and time

To be inventive

In order to achieve these aims, try to be receptive to new ideas and do not be afraid to experiment. Be aware of light in the world around, of all its illuminating qualities.

Research as widely as possible and make good use of practical experience. Always try to work closely with the production team and with the director.

The lighting designer's role

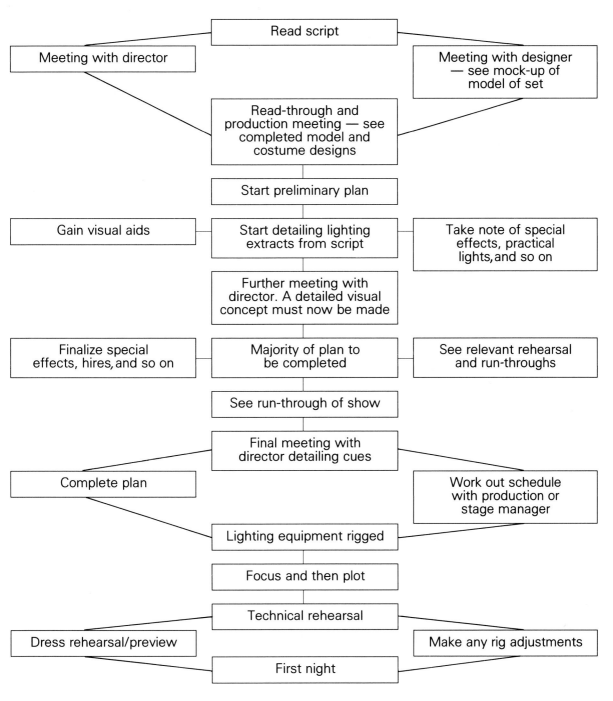

```
                          Read script
                              |
Meeting with director                    Meeting with designer
                                          — see mock-up of
                                          model of set
              Read-through and
              production meeting — see
              completed model and
              costume designs
                              |
                     Start preliminary plan
                              |
Gain visual aids      Start detailing lighting      Take note of special
                      extracts from script          effects, practical
                                                     lights, and so on
                      Further meeting with
                      director. A detailed visual
                      concept must now be made
                              |
Finalize special      Majority of plan to      See relevant rehearsal
effects, hires, and so on   be completed       and run-throughs
                              |
                     See run-through of show
                              |
                      Final meeting with
                      director detailing cues
                              |
Complete plan                               Work out schedule
                                            with production or
                                            stage manager
                     Lighting equipment rigged
                              |
                      Focus and then plot
                              |
                      Technical rehearsal
                              |
Dress rehearsal/preview                     Make any rig adjustments
                          First night
```

Equipment and basic techniques

In order to fulfil all the roles of the lighting designer, a thorough understanding is needed of all the equipment available and the necessary lighting techniques that can be used. The lighting designer can then light the actor and the stage, using design and illumination in a creative way.

It is therefore important to be familiar with the functions and particular merits of each piece of equipment that is likely to be within the experience of the designer concerned. This will obviously vary according to the size and budget of the theater or group concerned.

This chapter describes various luminaires that are available for theatrical use, their particular merits, their disadvantages, and how to focus and maintain them. Patching boards and control boards (both manual and computerized memory systems), along with lamps and dimmers, are discussed in sufficient detail to enable even a complete novice to appreciate their individual attributes and application.

The designer must then exploit this equipment to the full, and this can be achieved only by understanding the basic principles of lighting technique.

Front light, side light, back light, down light, up light, and silhouette; all these different ways of lighting the actor and the stage are fully explored, as well as the meaning of key and fill light. All this knowledge must be absorbed and put into practice before the designer can become truly expert.

Moreover it will be very difficult to communicate with the rest of the production team without this basic know-how. It is pointless to demand the impossible of electricians, control-board operators, or the equipment itself. At the same time, one's "vision" should not be cramped by technicalities.

Try to understand fully what is involved and then find the means to achieve your perception of the play, despite any limitations imposed.

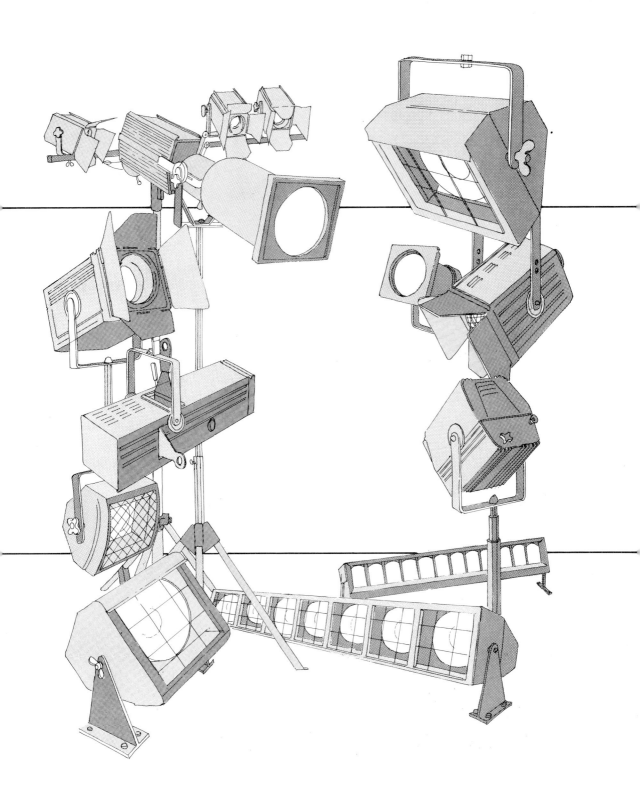

Luminaires

The range of lighting and equipment available for the theater today is enormous, and growing larger all the time, as new technology introduces new equipment.

Just a glimpse at the vast array of luminaires (or instruments) in a professional theater (or the number of pieces of equipment on a lighting plan) can be a daunting experience for the uninitiated.

However, there are many variations on a theme; it is really not as complex as it first appears. Basically, only five types of luminaire are regularly used and these are:

The Profile spot
The Fresnel spot
The Pebble-convex luminaire
The Par
The Flood

A beam light or projector, which is rather like a modified searchlight, might also be used.

The term luminaire merely means any lamp fitted within a casing — as opposed to a naked lamp. Within each type of luminaire, up to four wattage sizes are available, these normally being 500 watt, 750 watt, 1000 watt, and 2000 watt.

Choosing the right wattage size is very important, especially to the amateur, for two reasons.

The first, and most important factor to consider, is the number of luminaires that can be used with the available mains supply.

For instance, it is obviously possible to use twice as many 500 watt luminaires than 1000 watt luminaires on the same mains supply. So, if a large number of lights are required, this might be the better option.

◇ Whichever lights are chosen, it is essential to know all the limitations of the electrical supply and to always keep well within them. (See page 155.)

The second factor to consider is the relationship between the audience and the stage. In a theater where the audience is seated close to the stage, less light will be needed to reflect off the stage area than when the audience are farther away.

Having considered all the particular requirements of the play, as well as the limitations of the electrical supply and the proximity of the audience, now the attributes of all the different luminaires can be considered.

The profile spot
ellipsoidal reflector spotlight

The profile spot provides a hard-edged beam of light. This beam is of a fixed size, is very intense, and has minimum flare (or stray light) outside the beam. As a general rule, the narrower the beam angle, the greater the intensity of light produced.

1 Shutters
2 Plano-convex lens
3 Lens (tube) focus knob
4 Color-frame runners (holders)
5 Gate, with slot for irises and gobos
6 Flat-field/peak knob (lamp alignment)
7 Lamp and ellipsoidal reflector housing

This is achieved because the spotlight has a gate aperture placed between the light source and the lens.

The maximum amount of light available is collected from the lamp by the reflector and is then passed through the gate. This gate, and its built-in shutters, determine the profile of the beam. The light is then focused by a plano-convex lens (a lens which is flat on one side and raised on the other, as opposed to a convex lens).

Four separate shutters are built into the gate to allow shaping of the beam. Some profiles have an extra set of shutters, which are mounted away from the gate to provide a soft, out-of-focus beam.

Gate runners allow for the insertion of irises. These will vary the size of the circular pattern of light (like the f. stop of a camera).

Alternatively, a gobo (or cookie) can be inserted. This is a special cut-out slide or template which creates a pattern of shadows. It is very useful for creating interesting effects, such as broken light dappling through leaves, or rippling water.

The way light fills a beam can also be altered and this is called flat field or peak, respectively.

Flat field means that the light is spread evenly throughout the beam. Peak means that a larger amount of light is concentrated in the center of the beam.

Some profiles are designed to provide a beam of variable size. These luminaires have two lenses which can move independently of each other. One lens is used to vary the size of the beam ; the other lens adjusts the focus.

The profile spot is a very useful piece of equipment because it is particularly efficient.

Focusing profiles

The hard or soft edge of the beam can be focused by the movement of the lens (diagram 1 and 2). The beam size can be adjusted when the luminaire is one which provides a variable beam.

Vary the beam size with an iris to make it smaller. Shape the beam with shutters to create both hard and soft focus (diagram 3).

Use a gobo (or cookie) for texturing or for projecting an image (diagram 4).

The distribution of light across a beam can be altered. This is called peak or flat field adjustment.

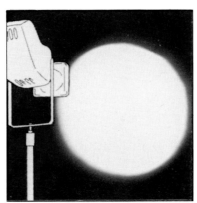

1 *A hard-edged beam*

2 *A soft-edged beam*

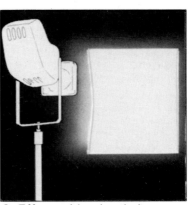

3 *Effect with a hard shutter used on the right, and a soft shutter on the left*

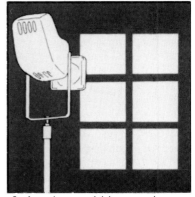

4 *A gobo could be used to project a window shape or whatever is required*

Luminaires

The Fresnel spot

The Fresnel spot takes its name from the Frenchman who originally designed the lens for use in lighthouses. At first it was mainly used by film studios and was rather expensive. Eventually, however, the price dropped and the Fresnel became more readily available. It is mechanically quite a simple instrument which produces a smooth wash of light.

The luminaire provides a soft-edged, ill-defined beam, which can be varied in size by moving the lamp and reflector towards or farther away from the lens.

The plano side of this lens has its surface cut away in steps to diffuse the light and is therefore called a stepped lens.

Unlike the profile spot, this luminaire has no gate. The luminaire is simply a box with a Fresnel lens at one end and a lamp and reflector which are both rigidly fixed to a plate. This plate can be made to slide along inside the box.

If beam shaping is required, a barn-door attachment can be fitted to the front of the luminaire. This usually consists of four independent doors or leaves, and can be rotated and angled to intercept and control the light.

These luminaires are ideal for lighting adjacent areas of the stage because the soft-edged beam means there will be no hard edges where the light beams merge. A small amount of flare exists outside the beam, but it is possible to lessen this

effect by using a colouvred lens. This lens has blackened steps (or risers) which reduce any stray light and eliminate flare.

Flare occurs because the light passes through the steps at such a shallow angle it creates a spectral flare or rainbow, just like the effect of light passing through a prism.

Fresnel spots are normally available in 500 watt, 1000 watt, and 2000 watt sizes.

Focusing the Fresnel

Vary the beam width by moving the lamp and reflector nearer to the lens for a bigger beam angle and farther away for a narrower beam angle.

Shape the beam of the luminaire with the barn doors.

It is easier to find the center of the beam if you first close the luminaire down to the smallest beam angle.

A Fresnel luminaire

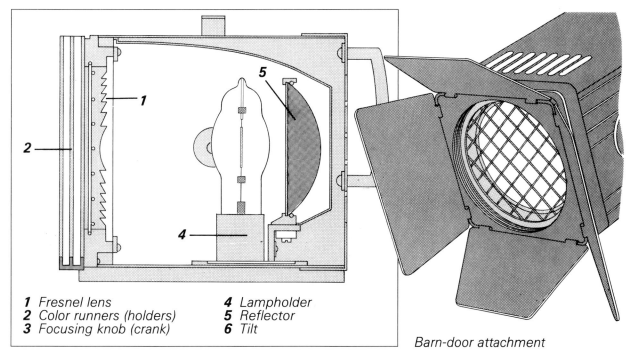

1 Fresnel lens
2 Color runners (holders)
3 Focusing knob (crank)
4 Lampholder
5 Reflector
6 Tilt

Barn-door attachment

The pebble-convex luminaire

Pebble-convex luminaires work on the same principal as the Fresnel luminaire, but this time the lens is a specially designed plano-convex lens. The back, flat part of the lens is stippled with bumps, which diffuses the light passing through the lens and makes the beam semi-hard edged.

These luminaires have no flare outside the beam. They are an excellent substitute for profile spotlights, if projection facilities are not required. The barn doors are used to shape the beam.

Focusing pebble-convex spots

Vary the beam size by moving the lamp and reflector nearer to the lens for a larger beam angle, and moving them farther away for a smaller beam. Shape the beam by using the barn doors.

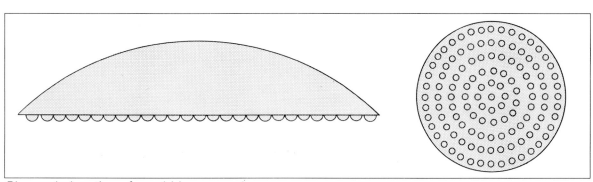

Plan and elevation of a pebble-convex lens

Luminaires

The Par

This luminaire provides an intense, virtually parallel, fixed beam of light and is rather like a car headlight. It consists of a lamp which has both a lens and reflector built into it. The luminaire shell is used to support the lamp and to keep flare to a minimum.

Pars are perfect for strong lighting effects such as bright sunlight through windows. Several used together on a batten (or border-light) can be useful as back or down light. A Par can also be an invaluable source of strong key light.

The lamps are 1000 watts, available in three beam widths; (9 x 12, 10 x 14, and 11 x 24 degrees) and 500 watts, which are available in four beam widths. Pars may also be available with 350 watt lamps.

Focusing Pars

It is necessary only to point the Par in the right direction, although because the beam is oval-shaped, it may be rotated.

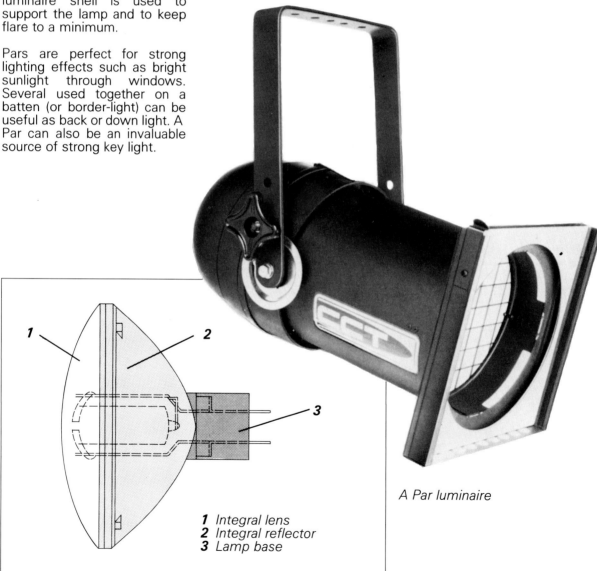

A Par luminaire

1 Integral lens
2 Integral reflector
3 Lamp base

Section of a Par lamp

The Flood
Reflector floodlight

As the name implies, floodlights are used to cover as large an area as possible, to flood the stage with light. They consist simply of a lamp and reflector, and are supplied with 150, 500, and 1000 watt lamps. By using several of these units together, it becomes possible to light large backcloths or cycloramas. A cyclorama is a curved or straight backcloth hung at the rear of the stage. It may be used as sky or background, painted white, and lit as required.

There are three types of floodlighting. The first provides an even distribution of light (see diagram 1).

The second type of floodlight provides more light at the bottom of the beam than in any other part. This is achieved by shaping the reflector in a complex way and using an epitaxial lamp, which is very long with a filament that travels along its whole length (as shown in diagram 2). These are excellent for lighting backcloths where the luminaire is rigged near to the top of the cloth, and when even illumination is needed from top to bottom.

The third type of floodlighting is on a batten. Several lamps with reflectors are fixed together in sections to form a strip light. When they are used on the stage floor, they are called ground rows: when used on the front edge of the stage, they are called floats or footlights. When battens are "flown" (suspended above the stage), they are known as magazine battens or border lights.

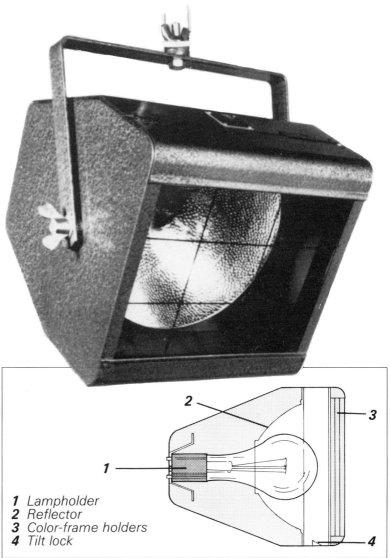

1 Lampholder
2 Reflector
3 Color-frame holders
4 Tilt lock

Section of a floodlight

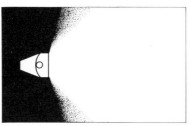

1 An evenly spread beam of light

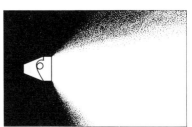

2 Light concentrated at the bottom of the beam

Luminaires

Ground-row batten

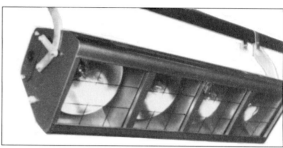

Magazine batten (border light)

Luminaire maintenance

Luminaires are very delicate instruments and should be handled, and stored, with care. Unless they are maintained in good working order, the reflector and lamp may slip out of alignment and the instrument will not stay in position properly. Nothing is more irritating than trying to focus badly maintained luminaires.

Moreover, any old or worn electrical equipment can be potentially dangerous and so, whenever possible (perhaps in advance of a forthcoming production), carry out these three simple maintenance checks on each luminaire.

◇ To avoid an electric shock, always remember to unplug a luminaire before attempting to maintain it.

1 Electrical check:

Check cable tails visually for splits or breaks.

Check the plugs: the colored wires should go to the correct pins and all the terminal screws should be tight.

The cable's outer insulation should take the strain in the cable sheath grip (or clamp) so that the electrical connections inside the plug are not put under stress.

Color coding for Europe

The green/yellow wire is connected to the terminal marked **E (earth)**. The brown wire is connected to the terminal marked **L (live)**, and the blue wire is connected to the terminal marked **N (neutral)**.

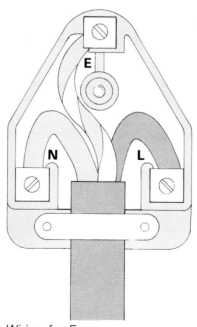

Wiring for Europe

Color coding for the USA

The black wire is connected to the hot (live) terminal. The white or natural gray wire is connected to the neutral terminal, and the green wire is connected to the safety ground (earth) terminal.

2 Optical check

Clean all the reflectors and lenses, and check that they are correctly positioned.

Make sure that the lamp is properly positioned in the lampholder and trimmed into alignment.

3 Mechanical check

Ensure that all the screws holding the luminaire together are tight.

Check that the tilt lock is working correctly.

Check that the lens tube and focus knob (crank) move freely.

Check that the shutters move freely but will remain where positioned.

Make sure that the lantern has a safety chain.

Lamps

Every luminaire needs a lamp to produce light. There are a bewildering number of lamps available, all with different wattage sizes and lamp bases.

The diagrams opposite show the fundamental parts of a lamp and the most common type of lamp bases used in theater luminaires.

Changing lamps

To avoid an electric shock, always unplug the luminaire before changing a lamp.

Remove a blown lamp with great care as occasionally the glass envelope can shatter. Grasp the lamp by the base, or hold it carefully with a soft cloth or a glove.

Always ensure the correct replacement lamp is used, as specified for the luminaire.

Do not forget to wear the plastic glove or shroud supplied with the new lamp. Never touch the glass envelope as any greasy moisture from your hands will attract heat and this could melt the glass, resulting in an explosion. If lamps have been touched, it is advisable to clean them with neat alcohol or methylated spirit.

Do not forget to remove the shroud when the lamp is correctly positioned in its lampholder.

Lamp bases

There are three types of lamp base most commonly used in theater luminaires but each type is available in two or three different sizes.

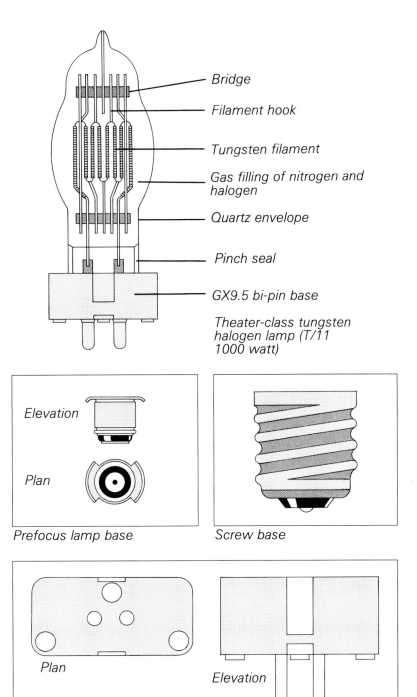

Bridge

Filament hook

Tungsten filament

Gas filling of nitrogen and halogen

Quartz envelope

Pinch seal

GX9.5 bi-pin base

Theater-class tungsten halogen lamp (T/11 1000 watt)

Elevation

Plan

Prefocus lamp base

Screw base

Plan

Elevation

Bi-pin lamp base

Dimmers

Control of the lighting during a performance is a fundamental requirement, and dimmers are the nerve center of any lighting control system. If the play requires a gradual transition from a black-out to full brightness (or vice-versa), dimmers provide the means to fade luminaires up and down.

The dimmers of today often use an electronic device called an SCR (silicon controlled rectifier). This device belongs to the thyristor family of semiconductor devices, which are simply switching devices. In order to fully understand the way dimmers work, some basic electrical knowledge is necessary (see pages 150-157).

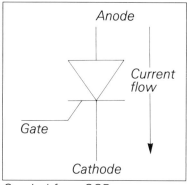

Symbol for a SCR

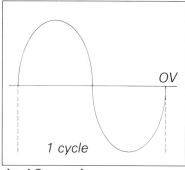

An AC waveform

The electricity supply consists of an alternating current. This means that the supply alternates above positive(+) and below negative(-) zero volts, making a complete cycle fifty or sixty times every second.

Two SCRs are required to control AC (alternating current), as current can pass only one way through them. Therefore, the pair of SCRs are wired "back to back", one controlling the positive (+) half of the cycle, and the other controlling the negative (-) half. With the fader at full (level 10), the AC waveform remains pure. This is because the SCRs are allowing full current to pass through by switching on at the start of each half-cycle. But, as the fader is brought down, then the point at which the SCRs turn on moves farther up the half cycle. This is called "phase control".

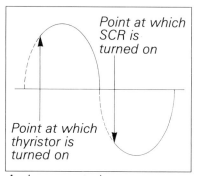

A phase control

SCRs can be turned off only by preventing the current passing through. This will happen automatically with an AC waveform, with each half-cycle starting at 0 volts, peaking to maximum, and then dropping back to 0 volts. Triacs are used in some dimmers and are similar to two SCRs.

Only one is needed to control an AC waveform. By using a trigger control to switch on the SCRs via the gate at the correct time, it is possible to regulate the current progressively, as required. The trigger control circuit is controlled by a "fader" on a lighting board.

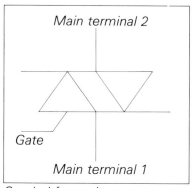

Symbol for a triac

Setting up dimmers

There are normally only two adjustments that can be made. These utilize either:

1 The relationship between the mains voltage at dimmer output and the control voltage from the lighting desk: fader at level 10.

2 The relationship between the reduced mains voltage at dimmer output and the control voltage from the lighting desk: fader at level 0.

These adjustments should only be made in strict accordance with the instructions from the manufacturer.

Note: Care must be taken with these two adjustments as the dimmers will be switched on while these checks are being carried out.

Manual preset lighting boards

Manual lighting boards provide a fader for each dimmer or channel, thereby allowing each dimmer to have its own independent control. To help the operator to fade a lighting state up or down, another fader, called a master, is used to control the level of output from each channel fader to its own dimmer. This collection of channel faders and a master is called a preset.

It is possible to set a lighting state on the preset without the lighting being seen on stage (with the master at level 0). Then, when a lighting cue is executed, the master is raised to level 10 (or full) and the lighting state is achieved on stage. At this point, if any more lighting states are required, channel faders will have to be moved during the performance by hand to modify the existing lighting. Add more presets, and several lighting states can be preset ahead and then played back by fading from one preset to another, using submasters.

Most manual boards have more than one master per preset. To avoid confusion, these can be labeled A or B, red or white, and so on. Above each channel fader is located a multi-position switch, which enables it to be switched to any submaster. This allows more than one lighting state to be set up on one preset, and is known as grouping. The manual board shown is a three-preset, three-group lighting desk or consul.

Using manual systems

As the channel levels have to be written down, it can be very useful to use a "dedicated" cue sheet (one which is designed for a specific lighting board), presenting a clear view of levels and grouping. On page 38 is a cue sheet designed for a thirty-six way, three-preset, two-group manual board.

A Rank Strand three-preset, three-group, manual–lighting control system

Manual cue sheet

Cue number

Time to be taken with movement of masters therefore state lighting change

Channel number

Production

Sheet number

channel level (F for full or 10)

Channel group switch position

When a previous preset is finished with, reset with a new lighting state

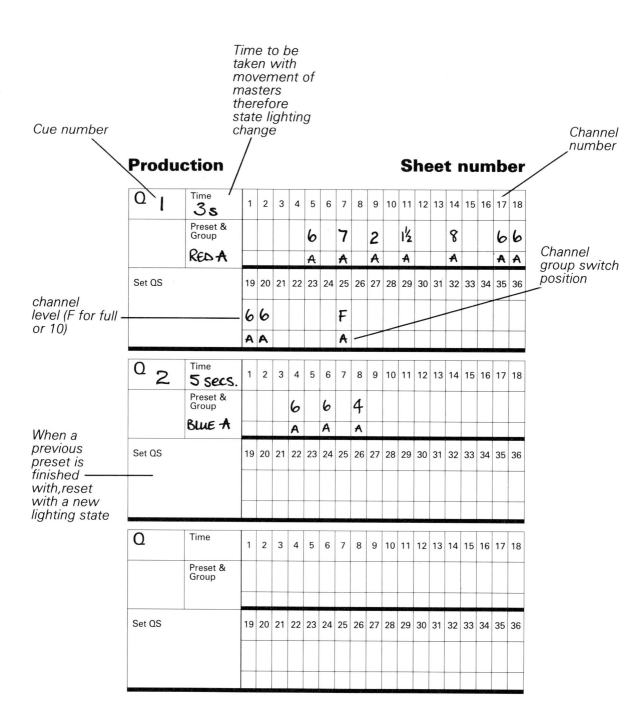

Typical cue sheet for a thirty-six way, three-preset, two-group manual board

Production
Sheet number

Q	Time	1	2	3	4	5	6	7	8	9	10	11	12	13	14	15	16	17	18
	Preset & Group																		
Set QS		19	20	21	22	23	24	25	26	27	28	29	30	31	32	33	34	35	36

Q	Time	1	2	3	4	5	6	7	8	9	10	11	12	13	14	15	16	17	18
	Preset & Group																		
Set QS		19	20	21	22	23	24	25	26	27	28	29	30	31	32	33	34	35	36

Q	Time	1	2	3	4	5	6	7	8	9	10	11	12	13	14	15	16	17	18
	Preset & Group																		
Set QS		19	20	21	22	23	24	25	26	27	28	29	30	31	32	33	34	35	36

Computer memory lighting control

Computer memory boards have revolutionized stage lighting techniques. The tedium of writing down detailed lighting plots is now removed and the whole process of lighting is quicker and more flexible.

Memory boards provide the facility to instantly play back a lighting state and reproduce it exactly, level for level. Also they can be used to fade or switch rapidly through many different lighting states, just as fast as you can push the buttons.

Moreover, a memory board saves a great deal of time during lighting sessions and rehearsals. Instead of writing down individual levels, one push of a record button will memorize the current lighting state and there is no need to wait for the board operator to set up possibly twenty or thirty faders. Entering a memory number and pushing a cross-fade button is all that is required to play back a lighting state.

Today memory boards are true computers, using computer memory RAM (random access memory) and floppy disks for storing lighting states, as well as cassettes or even cartridges.

As computers are purely digital devices, the output to dimmers is stepped. The more expensive boards can have over two hundred and fifty different steps between levels 0 and 10: the cheaper variety as few as thirty-two.

On slow fades, if the steps are too few, the audience may be aware of the switching of the dimmers through each step. This is obviously undesirable because the lighting will look jerky, so the more steps, the better the result.

The first memory system shown here is Rank Strand's "M24", which is eminently suitable for use in a small

theater, a school, or an amateur dramatic society.

It can control sixty dimmers and is able to memorize nearly two hundred different lighting states. Six different cues can be controlled simultaneously at different recorded speeds, and a sequence of over fifty timed cues can be automatically run in succession.

As well as memorizing all the lighting in this way, these control systems allow an operator to take immediate action if need be. The lighting on stage can be instantaneously altered if an operator or electrician chooses, so in no way need operators fear that the whole process has been taken out of their hands.

Obviously such systems are far more advanced than any manual board, and all the buttons and controls might

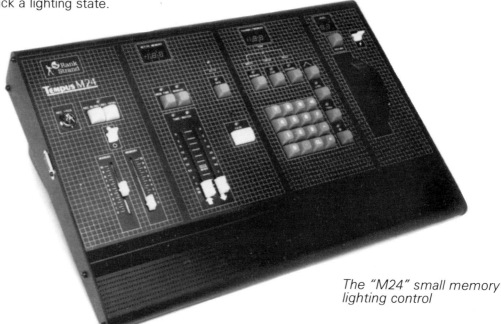

The "M24" small memory lighting control

seem rather confusing and complicated at first. They are, however, relatively simple to operate and the electrician will probably discover how to use the basic controls surprisingly quickly. As the whole thing becomes more familiar, he or she will be able to experiment with the more advanced refinements such machines have to offer.

In fact, once the electrician or board operator is able to fully exploit the new system, the whole process of a lighting rehearsal will be very much quicker. In fact, the lighting designer may have to adapt prevailing methods drastically in order to keep up!

Memory systems like these are quite small and so have the added advantage of being readily transported if the show goes "on tour".

As new developments and advances in the technology of lighting memory systems are taking place all the time, up-to-date information must be obtained from manufacturers before deciding which system will suit your needs and budget.

The other memory control system shown here is Rank Strand's top of the line "Galaxy" system, a rather more complex and expensive piece of equipment. However, a very wide range of systems is now being produced and small theater companies need not automatically assume that these systems will be beyond their budget!

Computerized lighting control systems represent the very sophisticated equipment which is available today. However, in order to create your own stage lighting, you will need to be familiar with the requirements of the particular stage you are planning to light, and with whatever equipment is already available there or within the budget to buy. Only then can you plan for future productions, and decide which control system is most suitable for your specific needs.

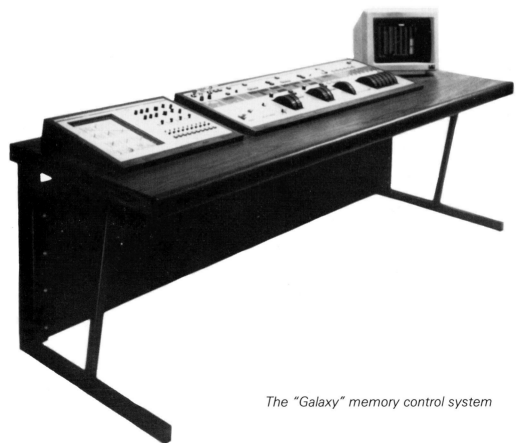

The "Galaxy" memory control system

Patching

In lighting circles, the term patching refers to a different system of "plugging up" the lighting, whereby a luminaire is plugged into a socket, which in turn is wired direct to a dimmer.

With patching, a luminaire is plugged into a socket. The socket is wired to a plug that fits into a patch panel. When required, this plug can be moved to a socket in the patch panel which is wired to a dimmer. This system is most commonly used in the USA, although similar systems do exist in England and Europe.

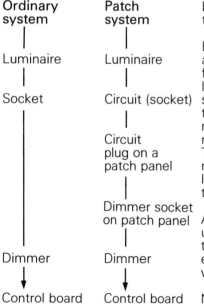

Ordinary system	Patch system
Luminaire	Luminaire
Socket	Circuit (socket)
	Circuit plug on a patch panel
	Dimmer socket on patch panel
Dimmer	Dimmer
↓	↓
Control board	Control board

At first this may seem an unnecessarily involved way of doing things. However, a well-designed patch system can save a great deal of time when cabling up luminaires. It can also make the whole process of "plugging-up" more versatile.

Take, for example, a small theater which has been wired up in the conventional manner with twenty-four dimmers and twenty-four luminaires. Each of the luminaires can be plugged into one of the twenty-four socket outlets around the theater. Each socket is then wired to one of the dimmers so that one socket is allocated to one dimmer. Imagine that twelve of these circuits or sockets are for the stage, and twelve for the front-of-house luminaires in the auditorium.

This, on the surface, appears to be a good workable system. The first twelve luminaires can be used on stage, and the other twelve for front-of-house.

However, should a situation arise when the set is built rather far to the front so that the lighting has to be set down-stage, then difficulties arise. All the luminaires may have to be rigged front-of-house and all may require separate circuits. This complication can be resolved only if twelve of the luminaires are cabled back to the socket outlets on the stage.

Although feasible, such an undertaking can be awkward, time-consuming, and also quite expensive as long cable runs will be needed.

Now imagine the same theater with the same number of dimmers and luminaires, but this time with a patch system. If the system incorporated forty-eight socket outlets in the theater, which were wired back to a patch panel, then there could be twenty-four sockets front-of-house and twenty-four on stage.

Any one of these forty-eight outlets could then be patched or plugged into one of the twenty-four sockets on the patch panel. These sockets, in turn, are wired to the dimmers.

Thus all twenty-four luminaires could be used with no problem, being either plugged on stage or at front-of-house. By patching on the patch panel, each can be allocated its own dimmer. This is just one example of the way the apparently complicated patching system can simplify matters. The complications are already "built-in" so to speak!

Patching is also useful for pairing. If two luminaires are required to share the same dimmer, but are on opposite sides of the auditorium, this can present a problem.

If, however, a patch system is being used, then the problem does not exist in the same way. The luminaires can be plugged to the nearest circuit and then they can be paired (or "ganged") at the patch panel. This can be done by plugging the two corresponding patch plugs into one patch socket, using a splitter (or adapter). Some patch panels will have a multi-socket arrangement for each dimmer in order to accommodate several patch plugs.

In some theaters the patch systems are so large that there may be literally hundreds of circuits. It is essential to keep track of exactly what equipment has been plugged and just how and where this has been done. Make a chart or keep a record (a hook-up schedule) of this, so that if any faults occur these can be dealt with quickly.

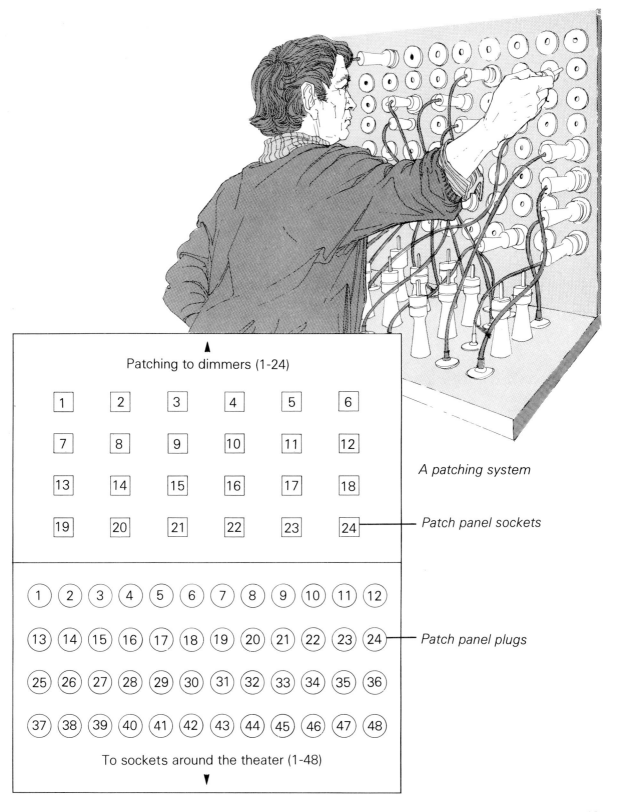

Patching to dimmers (1-24)

1	2	3	4	5	6
7	8	9	10	11	12
13	14	15	16	17	18
19	20	21	22	23	24

A patching system

Patch panel sockets

(1) (2) (3) (4) (5) (6) (7) (8) (9) (10) (11) (12)

(13) (14) (15) (16) (17) (18) (19) (20) (21) (22) (23) (24) — *Patch panel plugs*

(25) (26) (27) (28) (29) (30) (31) (32) (33) (34) (35) (36)

(37) (38) (39) (40) (41) (42) (43) (44) (45) (46) (47) (48)

To sockets around the theater (1-48)

Basic techniques

All the different luminaires discussed in the previous section are the tools of the lighting designer. Before they can be properly used to light the actor and the stage and to create a visual concept, the designer must understand the basic techniques of lighting.

Lighting structures

The way the light from each luminaire is made to fall upon the stage or an actor alters its structure fundamentally. Side light, top light, back light, and so on we shall refer to as lighting "structures". The manner in which these structures can change the appearance of people or objects on the stage means that light really can be used as a modeling medium.

Flat front light

If flat front light is used in isolation and shines directly into the actor's face, it flattens the features and looks very bland.

However, it is useful when an unavoidably high key light has made an actor's eyes disappear into the shadows cast by the upper part of the eye socket. This is when front lighting at a flat angle can alleviate the problem and is often used as an "eye-socket filler"! Never set the intensity level too high, or ugly shadows will be cast on the up-stage part of the set.

Front light at 45 degrees

Place the front lights at a 45 degree angle and they instantly become more flattering. This is the beginning of "portrait" lighting and also creates good cover for the acting area.

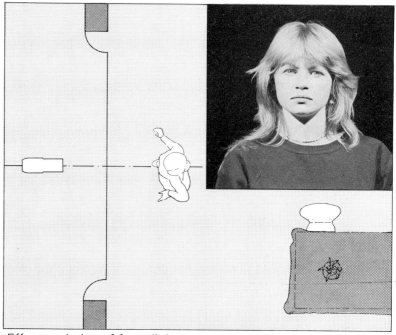

Effect and plan of front light

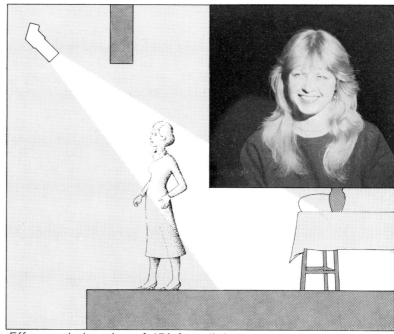

Effect and elevation of 45° front light

As a rule, the object of the exercise is to light the actor, particularly his or her face. To do this most naturally, a spotlight should be rigged approximately 45 degrees above and 45 degrees to the side of the actor's face. By using two spotlights, one on each side at this 45 degree angle, harsh shadows will be avoided.

Key and fill light

The terms "key light" and "fill light" describe the direction and intensity of the lights being used. A key light provides the main source of light in any scene and the fill light, appropriately, fills the areas of shadow that this main key light also creates. (See also pages 83-84.)

Side light

Side lighting may be considered the second most important structure to use when lighting an actor. Side light is created, more or less, as soon as the luminaire moves to one side of the vertical plane, above the actor or object being lit.

If the angle of side light used is very shallow or horizontal to the actor, then it may be termed "cross light". It will usually emanate from the wings of the stage, with the luminaires rigged on booms, ladders, or stands. If required, it can be made to cross the stage from one side to the other, without lighting the stage floor.

In general, side light helps to mold and sculpture the actor on stage. It lights the actor's face when he or she faces the wings. Without side lighting, or backlighting, the actor's face

would otherwise be plunged into shadow when turned away from the audience. Side light also makes a very useful key light. For instance, in a box set, a strong side light could be used at the side of the stage where a window is supposed to be, as though sun or moonlight is streaming in.

Side lighting at head height is sometimes used for special dramatic effects as it edges or "rims" the actor's body with light. This is particularly useful for dance or ballet. It does, however, look unnatural, and has the disadvantage that the performers may cast shadows upon each other.

Elevation of 45° side light

Effect of horizontal side light

Effect of 45° side light

Basic techniques

Back light

Back light has several functions. First it will add to the sculpturing qualities of a design. If there is a high proportion of back light above and behind the actor, the beams will create a halo on the head and shoulders. This helps to separate the actors from the background.

It should also be noted that back light will not affect an actor's face. This can be very useful when the stage needs to be heavily colored with a light which would normally alter the skin tones of an actor. By using the strong color as back light, and normal skin-tone colors for the front light, dramatic stage color changes can be made without turning the actor bright green or red! He will of course, have a colored "halo" on the head and shoulders, but this is acceptable.

The whole mood of a scene can be altered by the use of differently colored backlight washes, indeed, it is by the use of backlight that atmosphere can be created. Light is added from the front to light the stage so the actor can be seen.

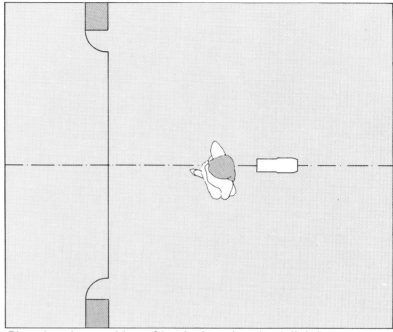

Plan showing position of luminaire when back lighting

Effect of back light

Back light shown in elevation

Top or down light

Top or down light should not be confused with back light. Although similar in its overall characteristics, top light will strike protruding body and facial features. It has excellent sculpturing qualities and is useful for high contrast work.

Because of its literally striking quality, the effect of top light can be quite dramatic. Lighting a fully-armored soldier from directly above will expose only certain elements of the costume: perhaps a protruding dagger or sword, or his breastplate and headgear.

The decision to use either top light or back light is therefore dependent on the design quality required.

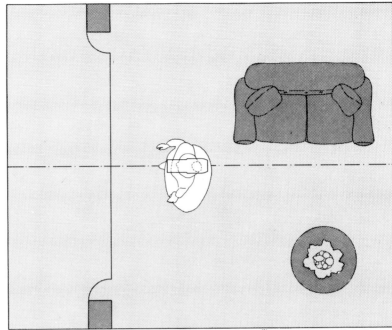

Plan showing position of luminaire when top or down lighting

Effect of top light

Top light shown in elevation

Basic techniques

Bottom or up light

Bottom or up light looks very unnatural and is rarely used today, unless it is the only way a particular special or dramatic effect can be achieved — such as actors grouped around a candle on the floor or sitting beside a camp fire.

Many years ago, bottom light was quite commonplace with the use of "floats" — so-called because the light here was once provided by oilwicks floating in water to lessen the risk of fire! Footlights (lights running across the front of the stage at floor level) can be categorized as bottom light.

Float positions can still be found in a lot of theaters today. These often consist simply of holes or slots in the forestage, normally covered with stage flooring. This flooring can be removed when the float position is required. The lighting designer is then able to insert lights to focus upwards, thereby lighting actors or scenery from below.

The effect of a single light uplighting an actor's face can be eerie and quite spectacular.

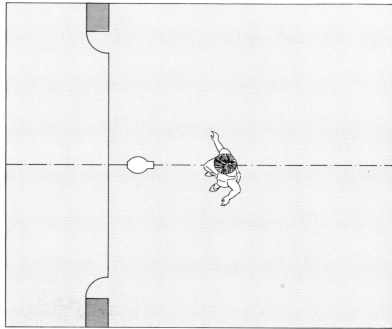

Plan showing position of luminaire when uplighting

Effect of up light

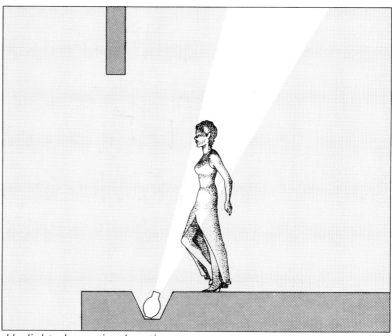

Up light shown in elevation

The use of a float batten (when several lights are fixed together) will give a more general and gentle up light. This is still used in some "old-fashioned" style productions — perhaps a Victorian melodrama, or a Restoration piece. The quality of this light will usually add authenticity to sets and costumes. Also, the color of the set or stage can be subtly altered by the use of subdued footlighting.

Pantomime is another type of production that may benefit from the use of floats. Scenic cloths can often take on a different character when lit from below rather than above.

Bottom light is also used to great effect to create an horizon, or perhaps a sunrise or sunset behind a scenic ground row. Because the most intense light is near the base of the cyclorama, a great illusion of distance can be created by lighting between a scenic ground row and a sky-cloth or cyclorama. A set designer will normally leave sufficient space between the two pieces of set to allow for this.

Ground-row sections usually come wired either in a two or three-circuit combination. It is possible, with several sections of ground row, to have a three-color wash from below on to the cyclorama (such as daylight, sunrise, and sunset).

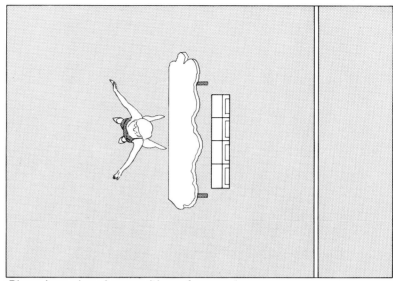

Plan view showing position of ground row

Ground row lighting shown in elevation

Sunset	Daylight	Sunrise	Sunset	Daylight	Sunrise	Sunset	Daylight	Sunrise

A three-color-wash ground row

Basic techniques

Silhouette

A silhouette, when required, is achieved by lighting just the background and nothing else. Obviously, unlit people or objects positioned in front of the background will then appear as dark outlines and shapes or silhouettes.

If the silhouette is to appear in front of a cloth or cyclorama, it is best to backlight the material, if possible, providing that the material is of the correct type. Back lighting prevents ambient light from bouncing around and will create a sharper silhouette.

It is not always necessary to light a solid background to create a silhouette. Back lighting a smoke screen behind an actor will create a stunning silhouette, with the image being "shadow projected" in the smoke. This use of shadow imaging is used a great deal in laser-light design.

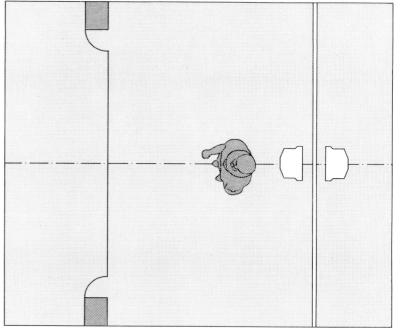

Plan showing position of luminaire for silhouette lighting

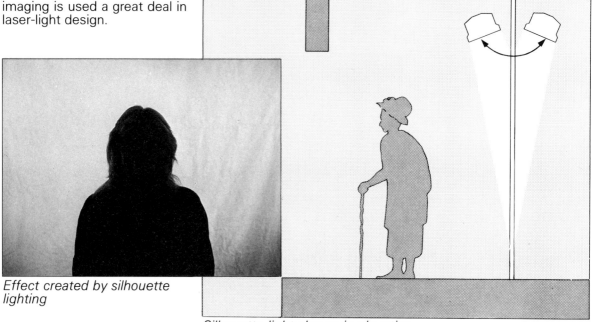

Effect created by silhouette lighting

Silhouette light shown in elevation

Stunning silhouette produced by using a back-lit smoke screen

Small beginnings

The lighting techniques which are discussed throughout this book will apply to all theaters, large and small, professional and amateur. However, the equipment that might be used to light the stage will vary enormously, and a very new or young organization with a small budget may consider that a great deal which has been discussed so far is beyond their capabilities or budget.

The chapter on *Lighting the stage with limited resources* explores many techniques that may be used to overcome some of these problems, and so make the most of what is available.

None the less, the beginner may well feel that some of the basic questions still remain unanswered. It is all too easy to assume that everything has been fully explained, to take for granted that everybody is fully conversant with the fundamentals and familiar with the normal lighting jargon. In this way the more basic but essential information may be overlooked.

Knowing just how to begin, finding out what is strictly essential for a first production, choosing, hiring, or buying new lighting, and then achieving a good result with perhaps as few as half a dozen luminaires; this is precisely the sort of information that is often sadly lacking but which the beginner needs to know.

Moreover the professional, too, might discover there is much to learn; a village hall or school production would probably be as daunting a possibility for someone used to sophisticated equipment as it is for the lighting "expert" who has just been coerced into lighting a play for the very first time!

Note: It will be useful to draw up a cue sheet for each production. There is an example of a manual cue sheet on page 39. In order that this may be photocopied, copyright regulations applying to the rest of the book have been released for that page.

How to begin?

What luminaires should the beginner choose?

It is not theater size alone which determines the choice of luminaire. Finances, lighting positions, power supply, and individual preference may well be the first considerations.

The Fresnel has an extremely versatile beam angle and is able to give a small "pool" or "spot" of light, or it can easily be "flooded" so as to cover a much wider area of the stage.

Profiles are also very useful when front-of-house positions are some distance from the stage. They are easier to control and will project gobos, which Fresnels are unable to do. Even so, their overall flexibility of beam angles will not compete with the Fresnel.

Some floodlights would also be very useful for cyclorama lighting and for lighting the stage behind the proscenium arch. They light a wide area of stage at a short distance, rather than providing a narrow beam of light, (although it should be remembered that the light from a flood is very uncontrollable).

Should footlights be used if they are already available?

Footlights should not be used simply because they are there. Certainly they can be used if the show particularly calls for them, perhaps for a Victorian music hall, a Restoration piece, or for lighting the curtain (the tabs).

Can luminaires be hired?

Luminaires may be rented but it is important to know exactly what is required. Contact the rental company in advance to inform them of your specific requirements and also tell them which alternatives would be acceptable (in case they cannot provide every item requested). Remember that insurance is very important. Most rental companies hold the customer personally responsible, so try to insure against every possible mishap, including accidental damage, theft, and fire.

What does up stage, stage right, and so on mean?

These expressions describe the geography of a stage. If an actor is positioned stage right, then, if seen from the auditorium, he or she will be on the left-hand side of the stage. The plan here shows all the different areas of the stage and the terms that are used to describe them.

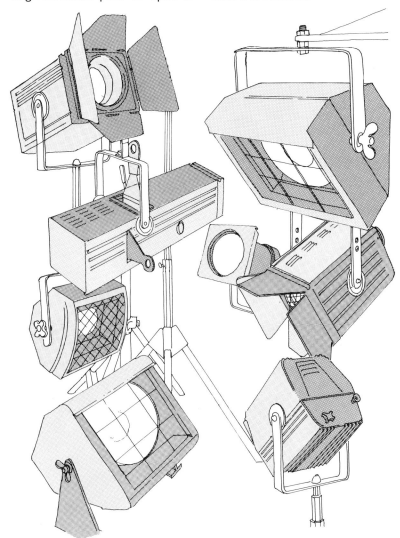

Cyclorama

EMIGRATING NEW YORK

Up stage right

Up stage center

Up stage left

Wings

Wings

Center right

Center stage

Center left

Wings

Wings

Down stage right

Down stage center

Down stage left

Areas of the stage

Avoiding accidents

How do you use safety chains and what are the legal requirements?

Safety chains should be fitted as a matter of course to all the luminaires. If the instrument is very heavy, make sure the chain is taut. A luminaire which is restrained by a slack chain would be badly jolted if it fell and this could cause breakage or might dislodge any fittings such as an iris or gobo. Legal requirements vary from city to city. Some authorities insist on safety chains being fixed to all luminaires hung above an audience. The Greater London Council rules that chains should be fitted to all luminaires. Always check local regulations, but in any event, use safety chains whenever possible.

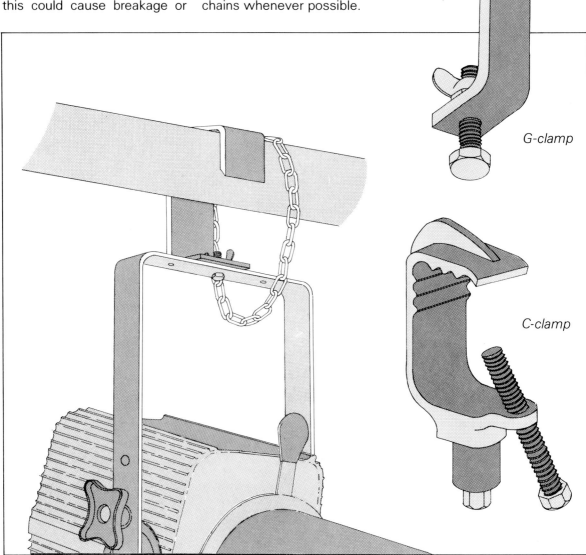

G-clamp

C-clamp

What ladders are best to use when rigging?

Use a new inverted Y-shaped ladder or a conventional A-shaped one. These are the most stable, but make sure they can reach the required height. Using an extending ladder will be rather dangerous if it is erected against movable scenery.

How do fire regulations affect lighting? Are lights on stands safe?

Again, fire regulations differ from city to city. Generally, aisles should be kept clear. If they are being used near the public, then the luminaires should be securely fixed or weighted down. This is something that should be discussed in the early planning stages with the production or stage manager and the fire authorities. Do not wait until the fit-up, when it may be too late to find another alternative.

Can insulation tape be used?

Insulation tape should never be used to splice power cables together. Always use proper connecting devices (preferably a plug and socket).

Are "bean-can" luminaires safe?

A bean or biscuit-tin luminaire is slightly vulnerable because it has such a thin frame or case. Avoid using these home-made lamps if they are likely to be kicked or could be knocked by heavy scenery. Normally they would not need a guard over the front. This is covered in greater detail on page 149.

◇ Are naked lamps a fire risk?

Naked lamps should not touch any scenery or drapes. Even though these items should be fire-proofed, a naked lamp, and even the luminaire itself, can become very hot and may singe even a fire-resistant material.

A Light collapsible stand with four telescopic tubes, each with wing nuts for securing

B Heavy-based telescopic stand with one extension

A

B

Using the luminaires

What is a follow spot and how is it used?

A follow spot is usually a profile spotlight which is operated manually to follow the actors, singers, or dancers on stage. It sits on a specially designed stand which enables it to achieve a smooth sideways movement. The spotlight will often have an iris to make the beam larger or smaller. It may also have a color magazine (to facilitate quick color changes) as well as some form of dimmer and black-out mechanism.

Most luminaires which are designed as follow spots have all these capabilities as part of their basic design. However, some of the arc-lamp follow spots (such as an HMI or Xenon carbon arc) cannot be dimmed from the light source but may be fitted instead with a mechanical dimming system which will provide this facility if required.

When using a follow spot with a light source other than tungsten it will be advisable to color-correct the light emitted back to that of tungsten. There are several filters which can do this, such as Lee 237 and Lee 238.

Follow-spots are expensive, so it is worth noting that any narrow-angle profile can be used as a substitute. It may be advisable to bolt a handle to the case of the luminaire as this can become very hot. The "follow spot" will then be much easier to manipulate. To control the size of the beam, put an iris into the "gate" and slide a piece of black card in front of the luminaire. This will then enable dimming or black-out to be successfully achieved.

How can you obtain the best results from just six or eight luminaires?

Providing that the basic rule of lighting is followed, (that is lighting at 45 degrees from the horizontal and vertical plane), then shadows should not occur. These are normally caused by using too low a lighting angle. Divide the stage up into a grid (rows and columns). Each section should be about one "light-pool" from corner to corner diagonally. (One "light-pool" is the diameter of the light spread from only one luminaire.)

In order to light the area in front of the proscenium arch and the downstage sections, four of the luminaires should be positioned in pairs at the ends of the front-of-house bar (pipe). Two further luminaires rigged on a bar behind the proscenium arch will light the upstage sections.

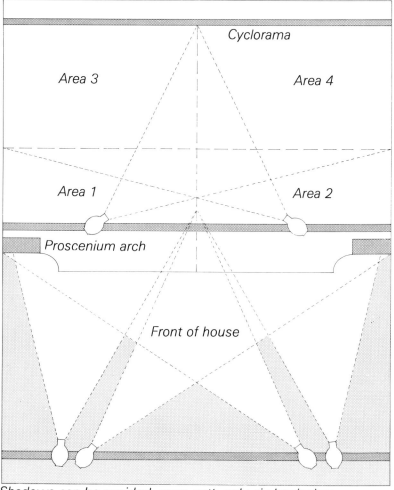

Shadows can be avoided, even with only six luminaires

Where should battens be?

The best place for a batten (strip light) is about one meter away from the cloth or border it is to light. If the batten is too close, then the shadows made by wrinkles or folds in the cloth may appear. If the batten is too far away, the intensity of light is lost and there will be light spill on the surrounding areas.

How many spot bars (pipes) are necessary?

There should be sufficient bar (pipe) space to support the luminaires needed for front lighting. Back and side lighting can be used for the remaining effects if space is at a premium.

How are luminaires masked?

The masking or concealing of luminaires is usually the set designer's task, but early meetings with the rest of the production team will help to achieve mutually desirable masking arrangements. Spot bars are often masked with borders and the designer will decide where to place these by working out the "sightlines", so that the bars are hidden, even to those sitting in the front row.

What is gauze and how is gauze used?

Gauze is a large-weave cloth which is useful for special effects (see page 121).

How is spill light avoided?

Light spill into the auditorium is usually caused by badly focused back light. A simple way to avoid this is to check the effect by sitting in the front

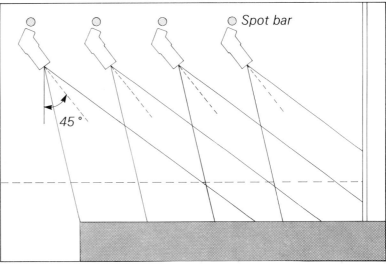

Four spot bars providing frontlight cover

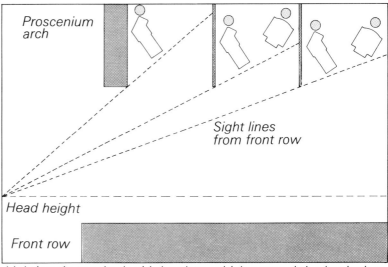

Lighting rig masked with borders which conceal the luminaires

row when the back light is focused. Then you can ensure the audience will not be blinded, and the shutters or barn doors can be adjusted to restrict the light to the stage edge. Ambient spill also occurs if front-of-house Fresnels are used from a position too far from the stage.

How is the auditorium lit?

House lights are normally part of the fabric of the building, but it is preferable to have two sets of lights: bright lights for normal use when there is no show (working lights), plus a set of lights that can be faded.

Color and special effects

What filters should be purchased?

Basic color will be needed for day, night, and so on. The choice will be dependant on the color of set, cyclorama, or backcloth that is being lit. Below is the list of Lee color numbers that may generally be used and should suit most circumstances:

Warm
Daylight: 103,159,212,206,205, open white

Cool
Daylight: 117,201,202,203,218

Moonlight: 143,161,174,183

Indoor:
103,151,152,153,154,162, open white

Street: as above (day/night)

Countryside/woodland: composite of ambers/golds

How are gobos used? Is it possible to make them?

Gobos can be used to project patterns and images, including tower-block lights, stars, or in fact anything you wish, on to a backcloth or curtain. Beware, however, as gobos can only be used in profile spotlights and have to be inserted between the lamp and the focusing lens, which is called the "gate". It is possible to make your own gobo. This is fully described in the *Special Effects* section.

Is projection possible?

Yes, projection can be used successfully in an amateur production. Normally a simple domestic projector will suffice but obviously, if used in a bright lighting state, it may not be bright enough. The use of slide projection has been covered in greater detail in the *Special Effects* section.

Can fluorescent paint be used? Are ultra-violet lamps legal?

Fluorescent paint will work effectively if used under ultra-violet light alone. Its use is quite legal, but if it is not available, fit a primary blue filter to a luminaire to provide a poor substitute.

Can lighting be a "substitute" for costumes or set?

This has been done in rock concerts and for some dance productions. Lighting may help to suggest time and locality, especially when the set is very basic. Perhaps, one day, lasers and holograms will be used to project sets.

How can lighting effect a scene change?

When stage hands are scene-changing, using break-up gobos would create a more interesting lighting state.

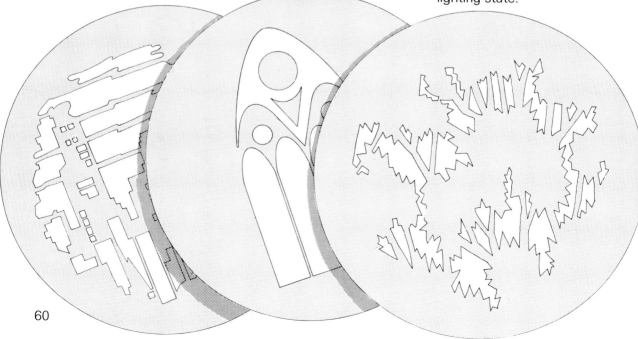

Problems and afterthoughts

How is a practical rigged?

A "practical", such as a table or standard lamp, should, when possible, be plugged into a circuit that is connected to the control board and not switched on or off by the actors on stage. In this way the required light changes can be co-ordinated.

How may a member of the audience be lit?

For lighting a member of the audience, a spotlight can be used. This must be pre-focused and is called a special (see page 84). To light someone entering the auditorium, a follow spot would be rather better.

What should the control-board operator do if an actor jumps six pages?

It is not the lighting designer's problem if several pages are suddenly omitted. The stage manager, or a prompt who has the book to hand, will advise or instruct all the relevant departments, such as lighting or sound, hopefully in a co-ordinated manner.

If a memory board is in use then this is no problem. The necessary memory, with its appropriate lighting state, can be readily called up and activated when the stage manager or prompt so instructs.

If a manual board is in use, then the operator will have to advise that he or she will require thirty seconds (or whatever time is necessary to set the relevant cue) and then inform them when it is set. Co-ordination with the person "on the book" and making sure clear and

appropriate cues are given will be vital at such moments if chaos is to be avoided.

How do you light the house tab (curtain)?

This is one situation where footlights would be ideal. If no footlights are available, then front lights positioned either side of the proscenium arch will suffice. At the beginning of the performance, any lighting of the house tab should be faded out slightly later than the auditorium lights, thus drawing audience attention to the stage.

How can a mirror be used without causing reflection problems?

Sometimes a small adjustment to the angle of the mirror will solve the problem. There is also a selection of low-reflective sprays on the market which will prevent glare. Alternatively the mirror can be lightly smeared with petroleum jelly or soap.

What are the most common lighting mistakes a beginner makes?

Often the beginner lights the set rather than lighting the actor. Reading the section on *Lighting the stage* (on pages 62-89) with its explanation of how to organize the lighting of the acting area, should be of considerable help.

Another common error is to frontlight with too much dense color. Tints should always be used for frontlighting.

Frontlighting a woodland scene in green — WRONG

Frontlighting a sunny day in strong yellow — WRONG

Frontlighting a night scene in very deep blue — WRONG

Therefore be careful with color and follow the guidelines in *Color* (pages 100-111).

Can one person successfully design and light a production?

John Bury designs and lights productions most successfully. A scenographer is the name usually applied to someone who is responsible for all aspects of stage design. In the United States, in fact, the areas of training often overlap.

Should smoking be permitted?

Smoking will not usually affect lighting but nowadays most theaters ban smoking for social reasons and because of the high fire risk.

What special or extra item should a company buy if left an unexpected legacy?

So much depends on the size and type of the company — it is difficult to generalize on this. It would be best to consult with the various manufacturers and exploit their knowledge to ascertain the requirements of a particular theater.

As these questions and answers show, there are not necessarily any "hard and fast" rules to follows. Often it is a case of preference or conditions imposed by the venue, but a great deal of fun can be gained in finding the solution.

Lighting the stage

Pre-planning

To light any production in a pleasing way and to achieve all the effects that the lighting designer, the set and costume designers, and the director require, and at the same time to be well organized, takes considerable time and thought.

Ideally, the lighting plan should evolve and grow from the early pre-planning stage, in order to contribute most effectively to the production.

Strangely, it comes as a surprise to some people that every luminaire used in a lighting rig will have been pre-planned before the production is really under way. It is not simply a case of rigging up any instrument into any available space and hoping you will have enough of both. Each luminaire will have its own place and its own specific job to do.

When in a professional situation methodical pre-planning is vital, and the lighting designer will have a much easier job if the set is co-ordinated in the initial stages to incorporate the lighting. The cost of re-rigging is often expensive and is always time-consuming.

So, for many weeks, the lighting designer will be sitting at a drawing board, working in plan and elevation (a cross-section plot of the stage, showing the height of the set and the lighting equipment). Thus the lighting designer ensures that when a luminaire is chosen for a job, its projection will not be blocked by borders or scenery and the light will cover all the area required. It would be ideal if there was also a model of the set to hand.

Initially, of course, the lighting designer must read the script and analyze it from a lighting point of view. Then he or she will be ready to discuss the production.

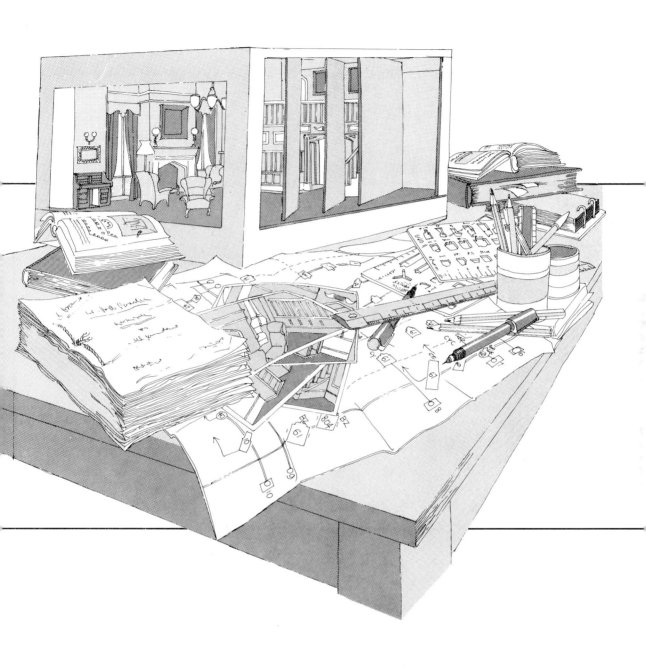

63

The early stages

Script analysis

The starting point of any production for the lighting designer should be a thorough analysis of the script. Even from a first, brief reading, many ideas will spring to mind. Certainly, the more obvious lighting demands should become clear and these will be the first to note, so jot down all the following information:

The time of day (such as morning, night, dusk, or dawn); the general mood of a scene (such as bright and amusing, or rather sombre and serious); and the more obvious lighting cues (lights being switched on or off, blackouts, and so on):

Exactly how the scene is lit; either artificially, by "practical" lamps — that is a light on the set which actually operates and is not merely decorative; or by natural daylight; or by a totally abstract form of illumination, such as might be used when lighting a musical.

Finally, if a scene is to be lit by artificial light, then record the source, such as electric light, candles, an open fire, gaslight, torches, and so on.

All this basic information is easily accessible from a first reading of a script and will at least give a broad outline of lighting requirements.

To illustrate how to examine a script rather more closely, Professor R.A. Shakespeare of Indiana University has provided the following description of a play, as analyzed by one of his students.

The Zoo Story
by Edward Albee

Zoo Story is a play about two characters, Peter and Jerry, and through them illustrates the desperation of contemporary man. It demonstrates his isolation within the community and his impotence inside the strictures of its culture and the social-economic system.

The characters of Jerry and Peter may often be seen as fragments of one single personality. Their union hardly forms a well-rounded human being but they do create a modern, masculine image.

The play does not offer any real hope; having made desperate attempts to extend beyond himself, to communicate with the outside world, and with Peter in particular, Jerry is killed. Peter is left as a terrorized, completely wounded character. Their tragedy is unresolved.

These two separate characters, and the unstable whole man they occasionally create, must be reflected in the approach to the lighting.

To illustrate this concept, Jerry and Peter should be kept in their own distinct realms of light, having moments when they come close, and only fully uniting when Jerry impales himself on the knife Peter is holding. Only occasionally should this emphasis be so jarring that it is consciously perceived by the audience, so the lights must not overshadow the characters.

No attempt should be made at naturalism; the stage should not be given the actual appearance of Central Park on a summer Sunday afternoon.

Cue sheet

However, the light may move from a color selection of amber tones at the start, to blue and magenta while the play progresses, culminating in an increasingly disturbed mood at the end of the drama when these two people are beyond the grasp of the rational. The light simply cannot have the warm beauty of sunshine and a park. It is not a pretty play.

Jerry represents, more often than not, the cruelty of man. He is subversive and fierce. Peter, on the other hand, represents what could be considered kindness; he is passive and accommodating. Therefore the edges of Jerry's light must be quite hard, and hot colors are needed to give clarity to the seething nature of his personality. The lighting for Peter should be less focused, impressionable, and pastel.

Cue sheet

Note: "Void" means negative space and emptiness

House down to level one to two in 7 count, hold 3 count. House out in 5 count

Q1 page 11
Stage lights up after Peter enters and takes his place on the bench.

SEE: Bench area surrounded in light, therefore separated as an island from the rest of the stage which is void-line. Bench area floor to be textured.

Q2 page 11
SEE: As Jerry enters, island delineation disappears, spreading the texture out across the stage.

Q3 page 12
Jerry: "Mister, I've been to the Zoo."

SEE: As Jerry approaches, stops, yells, island forms again. For the first time we see Jerry sharply focused against Peter's less-defined features.

WHY? This space has opened up to let Jerry in, encapsulating him alone with Peter. Initial contact indicative of their entire encounter — Jerry's aggression to Peter's off-guard reception.

[Follow on]

SEE: Balance in their respective states of brightness as conversational tone is taken.

WHY? So the audience anticipate quickly the intensity of this relationship.

Q4 page 16
Jerry: "But you wanted boys."

SEE: Peter's color change to take on a highlight of the void color.

WHY? Sense the depth of Peter's powerlessness, impotence. Atmosphere: chilly, disquiet.

Q5 page 19
Jerry: (remembering) "Wait until you see the expression on his face."

SEE: Jerry in a cloud of color. Peter returns to normal pastel state.

WHY? Jerry in another world.

Q6 page 20
Jerry: "The Zoo?"

SEE: Jerry return to his previous state.

WHY? Because he has returned to the present.

Q7 page 21
Jerry: "It's one of those things a person has to do...correctly."

SEE: Jerry moves to Area III.

WHY? As he moves the light will come up on an area, falling again once he is no longer there. So illumination bursts into life and then dies — open, then close.

Q8 page 21
Peter: "Oh, I thought you lived in the village."

SEE: Peter's image flattens out.

WHY? Dulled senses.

Cue sheet

Q9 page 24
Jerry: ".... and I have no feeling about any of it that I care to admit to myself."

SEE: Brief dip in Jerry's brightness, Peter less flat.

WHY? Like a sigh, fatigue.

[Return to previous lighting state Q8]

Q10 page 25
Jerry: "I never see the pretty ladies more than once, ...camera."

SEE: Jerry in void shade, slightly redder. Peter no longer flat.

WHY? Cannot sustain, cannot build, brittle, mean.

Q11 page 27
Jerry: But I imagine you'd rather hear about what happened at the Zoo."

SEE: Jerry's previous color comes back, red returning.

WHY? Break, return to first subject.

Q12 page 30
Jerry: "What I mean is animals are indifferent to me...time."

SEE: Jerry's brightness goes up slightly.

WHY? Indifference? Animals?

Q13 page 31
Jerry: "Don't react, Peter; just listen."

SEE: Peter momentarily brought up brighter. Floor starts to lose gobo effect.

WHY? Attention, Self-conscious, flush..."kill?"

[FO Peter's light goes back to old brightness. Jerry in Area I.]

Q14 page 32
Jerry: "People looked up."

SEE: Peter goes slightly dimmer.

WHY? Absorbtion, suggests the adrenalin pulsing!

Q15 page 34
Jerry: "I had tried to love, and I had tried...themselves."

SEE Peter back to normal illumination. Jerry begins to go brighter, color vivid.

WHY? Understanding, realization.

Q16 page 35
Jerry: "I have learned that neither kindness...emotion."

SEE: Full realization of Jerry's light state.

WHY? Clear, bright, hot.

Q17 page 36
(Silence)

SEE: Jerry hollowed, shadow effect as he sits.

WHY? Past his peak, burnt out.

Q18 page 39
Jerry: ".... to find out more about the way people exist with animals,.....too."

SEE: Peter growing less muted. Floor texture goes.

WHY? Pressure, surface tension, descend.

Q19 page 43
Peter: "I feel ridiculous."

SEE Void color comes up on Peter, a bit sharper. Rhythmic progression, coming together in their respective light states.

WHY? Distortion, blows of frustration.

Q20 page 44
Jerry: ".... is this your honor?"

SEE: Step 2, both with touches of void color.

WHY? Punctuation, goading.

Q21 page 45
Jerry: "Like a man?"

SEE: Step 3

WHY? Holding

Q22 page 47
(With a rush he charges Peter and impales himself on the knife.)

SEE: Same light, both in Area V. Hollow, sharp, other world envelops around figures, void color closing in on island.

WHY? Union, futile.

[FO Moving apart: Peter now hollow and increasingly less focused. Jerry less bright, already becoming wrapped in another world.]

Q23 page 49
Peter off-stage, Jerry on bench. Entire stage in void color.

WHY? Frigid pain.

House lights to level one to two in 7 count, hold 3. House lights up full in 5 counts.

Solving lighting problems

The discussion stage

All too often, unfortunately, the lighting designer is invited to join the production team's discussions when the set has already been designed and a model of it built — a *fait-accompli!*

Therefore, if there are any major problems with lighting the set, it is often too late for the design to accommodate certain lighting requirements.

The lighting designer will then have to solve the problems some other way. There have been a number of productions when a particular lighting position has been impossible to accommodate, and light has had to be bounced off mirrors and back into the set. It is often necessary to compromise, so the sooner the lighting designer becomes involved, the better. All aspects of the production are more readily adjusted in their early stages.

Assuming that the lighting designer has already studied the script, this first meeting will be the next stage in discovering just how the show is going to be lit. This is usually the time when the model of the set is presented, with or without its inherent problems.

Further discussions with the production team, as well as the director, should soon take place. The ideas of all concerned need to be assimilated, especially the director's vision of the production, until eventually the various concepts will, hopefully, all "gel" together. Then the planning of the lighting rig can really start.

Problems to be discussed

Early consultation with the set designer and director will add to the basic information gleaned from the script. With this in mind, and an inspection of the model of the set (this may be just a white cardboard "mock-up" at this stage), various problems may arise.

Awkward areas

The best lighting sites are not always available. For example, when a projector is required, time and again the lighting designer discovers that the set design prevents the projector being accommodated in the ideal position, which can often be the case if the projector is a very large one. A mirror must then be used to reflect the image to the required position. Mirrors are very useful; they often come to the rescue when a lighting position is awkward.

An open (or exposed) rig

A general discussion may take place to decide whether or not the rig should be open (unmasked). If it is open, the design will have no borders and the luminaires will be visible. However, with a little ingenuity, the lighting rig can be designed to be incorporated as part of the set and shaped to enhance the overall concept, while still remaining a practical vehicle for the lighting design.

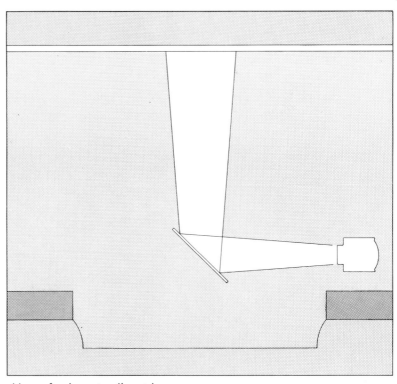

Use of mirror to divert beam

Solving lighting problems

Ceilings

When a lighting designer is first handed the model of a set, two important questions about the design are immediately answered: Is it a box set? Does it have a ceiling?

A ceiling severely restricts the lighting positions available on the stage. It is altogether easier, from a lighting point of view, if the ceiling is "suggested" rather than a permanent feature. At this point, however, it is not too late for the lighting designer to ask for a few concessions. If it can be masked, a niche might be cut into the ceiling piece to accommodate a lighting bar.

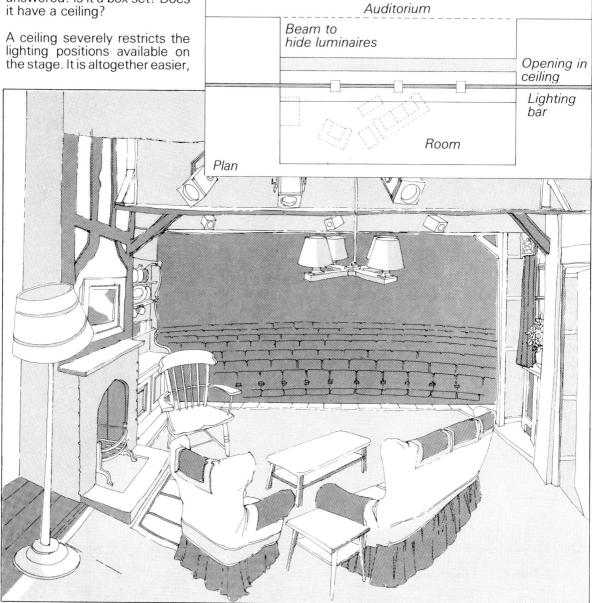

Lighting bar set into niche and masked by ceiling beams

Accomodating side light

Side (or cross) light may be essential to a particular lighting plot. If this is the case, then the sides of the set staging must be able to accomodate all the ladders, stands, or booms which the lighting designer will need to use.

(A boom, or light tree, is a vertical barrel or pipe, which sometimes has "arms", and which has a heavy base. It is bolted and secured at the side of the stage where it supports luminaires for side lighting.)

The ideal situation in which to place these lights is behind side flats or legs. (Legs are vertical curtains or scenery which are hung to mask the sides of the stage from view.)

Lighting booms or ladders can then be sighted immediately up stage of these structures. If possible, the masking (whether flats or legs) should be angled so that the on-stage edge is turned very slightly down stage, towards the audience.

At this angle, the masking will create its own shadow and prevent any light which crosses the stage from one side to the other from splodging all over the masking on the opposite side.

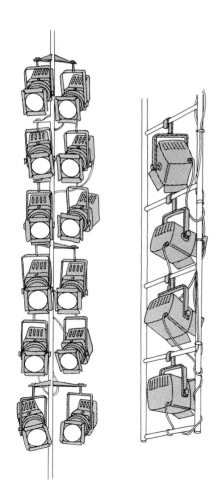

A boom or light tree and a lighting ladder

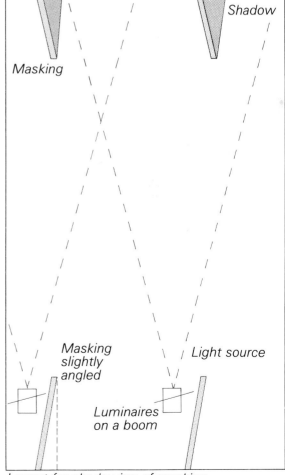

Layout for shadowing of masking

Solving lighting problems

The Cyclorama

The set designer may have chosen to use a wrap-around cyclorama. (This means that the cyclorama is, literally, wrapped around the sides and the back of the stage.)

At first, it might appear to be impossible to incorporate any lighting positions from the side with this arrangement. It is, however, still possible to use side lights with a wrap-around cyclorama, provided this can be "doctored" a little.

The best method is to "tent" the cyclorama. The material at the bottom half of the "cyclorama" is split in a vertical line and separated to form a "tent", behind which lighting booms can be hidden.

A conventional untented wrap-around cyclorama will not permit light to enter the set from the side, whereas a tented wrap-around cyclorama will allow the use of side light. If the tenting is carefully placed, most of the audience will be unaware that it exists.

All these potential problems, which can arise from the particular demands of the production in hand, should be thoroughly investigated and discussions held as soon as possible. Difficulties and conflicts may arise later if these basic problems are not resolved in the early pre-planning stages. Hopefully, the production team will develop an understanding of each other's needs and of the play as a whole.

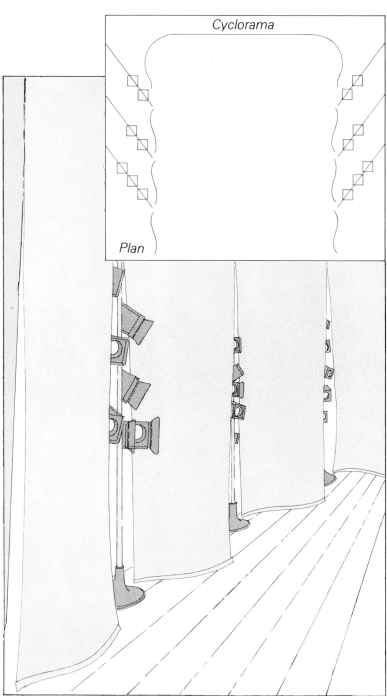

A tented cyclorama

The model of the set

The director and the lighting designer should use the early discussion stage to express their views about the set with its designer. Hopefully, any major problems can be resolved at this time. Then, when at last everyone is happy with the basic ideas, a full model of the set will be completed by the set designer to encompass these.

This model will be a much more detailed product than was the first white cardboard "mock-up". It will represent the set and all the scene settings, painted and decorated so that they appear exactly as they will on stage — only in miniature.

When the model is complete, the lighting designer will then have a very clear picture of how the show is going to be staged.

The most widely-used scale is one to twenty-five (1:25). This means that the set will eventually be constructed and painted exactly like the model, only now it will be twenty-five times bigger!

Other scales that may be used:

one to fifty (1:50)
one to twenty (1:20)
quarter inch to one foot ($\frac{1}{4}$": 1 ft)
half inch to one foot ($\frac{1}{2}$": 1 ft)

Model of the set for The Gondoliers

The lighting plan

The ground plan

At this point, the set designer may also produce a ground plan. This plan will represent the exact layout and position of the set on the stage, just as the model did but this time in two dimensions. It will be drawn to exactly the same scale as the model was constructed. This will avoid any confusion over measurements and generally makes life easier when it is necessary to look at the model and the plan side by side.

On occasions, the lighting designer may be lucky enough to be given the first choice of lines (line sets) but this is not often the case. Invariably the lighting designer can use only the flying lines that are still available and have not already been allocated elsewhere.

So it is very important to make full use of the early production meetings to discuss the lighting needs with the set designer. Then the lines can be allocated to best suit all concerned. Compromises can be made, such as the moving of a border to facilitate a better lighting position. In this way, the lighting designer should be able to set about the marking up of the ground plan without feeling too restricted and frustrated. His ideas have already been taken into account.

Reproducing lighting structures on paper

There are, of course, various forms of light angles and positions which can be used. These will be referred to as "lighting structures" (see also pages 44-50).

Front light, side or cross light, back light, bottom or up light, top or down light, and silhouette — all these are potential lighting structures.

Each will be selected for its own special characteristics. Very often, a number of different lighting structures will be used together. However, if used in isolation, most structures can be very dramatic; up light is always particularly effective.

Each lighting structure has its own way of being represented on a lighting plan and elevation. It is important to understand how this is done in order to make full use of this early planning stage.

The lighting designer, having explored the possibilities of all the available lighting structures, has to represent them on plans and elevations in this manner. By doing so, all the ideas are properly recorded so they can be readily discussed, and will be planned in an organized way.

Using symbols on the plan

The equipment chosen by the lighting designer will need to be represented on the lighting layout plan. The set designer will normally supply a master plan showing a bird's eye view of the stage.

The layout of the set design will already have been incorporated on to this plan. The lighting designer's first task is to indicate on it the lines of the bars, or pipes, on which all the lighting equipment will be hung in place.

The designer will then enter on to these lines a symbol to represent each piece of equipment that is required. It is quite in order to devise a personal system for this, provided the chosen patterns are always drawn to scale, consistent, and can be clearly understood by means of a key.

Alternatively, stencils can be purchased which provide highly accurate representations of individual pieces of equipment. These are made of beveled plastic and are similar to the stencils used to help students draw chemistry equipment. They are, however, rather expensive, but well worth the outlay as the accuracy of their scale enables the designer to judge exactly how each luminaire will fit the available area especially important if space is at a premium.

If these stencils are beyond your budget, a good compromise is to use a set of symbols that is already widely used and will therefore be easily understood by others who may need to look at the plan.

One such system is illustrated on the right:

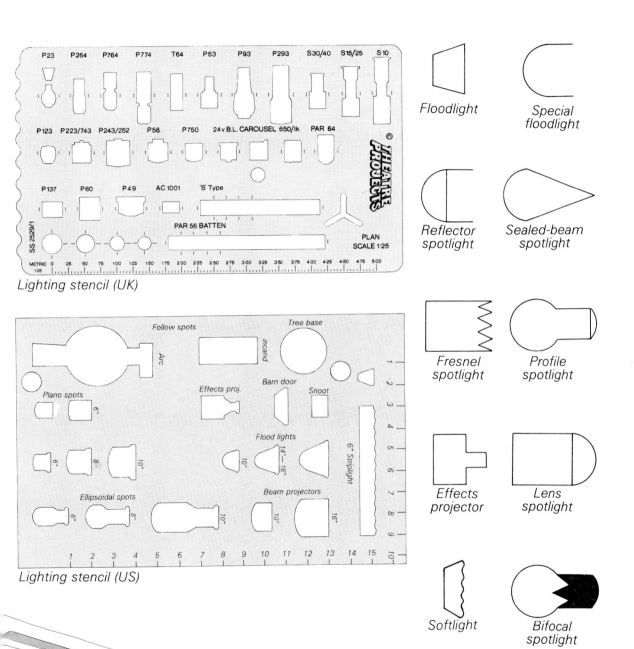

Lighting stencil (UK)

Lighting stencil (US)

Floodlight

Special floodlight

Reflector spotlight

Sealed-beam spotlight

Fresnel spotlight

Profile spotlight

Effects projector

Lens spotlight

Softlight

Bifocal spotlight

The lighting design

Further discussion

Before the luminaires can actually be placed on the plan, the lighting designer will probably find that more information is required. The study of the script and the general ideas about the play obtained at the first meeting will now need to be augmented by more serious consultation with the director.

It should not be forgotten that by now the lighting designer will have formulated a far more definite idea of how the play is going to appear to the audience, of its visual impact. So now is the time that the finer points of the design will need to be considered.

If special effects are required, they will almost certainly need to be considered at this time too. This subject is discussed separately in *Special effects* (pages 112-141).

Hopefully, the set designer will also attend this consultation. Using the model to illustrate what is actually happening, the show can be analyzed, scene by scene. Each person has a chance to make suggestions, and the lighting designer should use this opportunity to try and blend all these different ideas into a central design.

Ideally, the design should fulfil all the directorial concept requirements, enhance both the set and the costumes, and also include the lighting designer's own vision of the production. Every show will reflect the work you have contributed and may even bear your own personal "stamp".

At the same time, it must be remembered that the lighting design has to be a team effort. These meetings are essential because the designer cannot work successfully in isolation.

Hopefully, the result of all these consultations will be a unified show — a carefully blended combination of all the elements of production.

The first rehearsal

If possible, the lighting designer should always try to attend the first day of rehearsals. This is when he or she will have an opportunity to hear the play being read through by all the members of the cast.

It is surprising how much information can be gained simply by listening to the actors as they read through the script. Certain moods, that are not at all apparent during an isolated study of the silent script, suddenly emerge in the spoken word. These changes of mood should be noted straight away because it may be decided to accentuate them by means of the lighting design.

Planning the rig

By now the lighting designer should be ready to start planning the rig on paper, to turn all the ideas and discussions into plots, plans, and elevations, using a set of symbols.

Rarely will the designer have a completely free choice of equipment. Instead, it is usually necessary to work within a particular budget or to utilize only the theater's own set luminaire stock.

So it is absolutely vital to make a careful choice of equipment which can do all that is required and achieve the desired effect. How lovely it would be if a lighting designer could always choose all the luminaires and equipment he or she would like best, with a completely free hand. However, such an ideal situation seldom occurs!

In any event, whatever the budget, each piece of lighting equipment must be selected for its optical characteristics. This information is contained in the chapter on equipment (see pages 26-51).

How to approach the lighting design

Each lighting designer has his or her own way of approaching a new lighting design. Much depends on the type of production. For instance, the way to start work on a musical, which requires a good many follow spots, would probably be

quite different from the approach to a serious drama.

Generally, however, it is best to start by working out how to light the acting area. If this is well covered and lit in a structured way, so that all the areas of light can be controlled, you are well on the way to creating a technically well-lit show. This must be achieved first and foremost. The design element of the lighting can then be taken into account.

Choosing the lighting structure

In order to light the acting area (often referred to as AA), many different lighting structures may be used. Careful consideration must be given to the properties of each potential structure and how it might be used in the production (see pages 44-50).

It is possible to combine several structures. Back light and front light might be used together, or front light and side light might make a useful combination. Perhaps the drama of the situation would be better highlighted by a single lighting structure. Down light or bottom light, used alone, may give the required effect. Do not necessarily determine to have the first and most obvious lighting structure which leaps to mind. Do explore all the possibilities.

Dividing the acting area into sections

Once the ground plan has arrived, it is useful to have a means of dividing the acting area into workable proportions. Then each segment of the stage can be allocated its own luminaires, and note taken of whether these are to be used for front light, back light, or whatever structure has been decided upon.

How the stage is to be divided will depend on a number of different factors:

1 The size of the stage
2 The shape of the set
3 The quantity of equipment that is available

All these elements must be taken into account on the lighting plan.

As a general rule, it is usually most convenient to split the stage into nine segments. Divide the acting area by three lines that go across and three lines down. This division of the stage will make a good starting point from which to work out the details of the lighting layout.

Each of these nine sections can now be treated as a little stage in its own right. Each should have its own 45 degree front

light. Perhaps each might also have its own back light, side light, or down light.

In this way, the lighting of each area can be carefully controlled and the illumination of the stage as a whole is far more manageable. It is then possible to ensure that the acting area receives good even cover and that the actors are well lit, no matter where they move to on the stage.

Divide the stage into suitable segments and light each area

Labeling the acting area

Before any decisions can be taken about how to light each of the sections, they must be given names by which they can be referred to individually, otherwise there will be terrible confusion at a later stage.

Each segment should therefore be clearly labeled on the plan. Then every luminaire can be marked with its appropriate focus point.

The method of labeling each area is very much a matter of personal choice. However, the lettering used in the diagram on the right has much to recommend it.

In the first place it is a very logical system. Moreover, once you are familiar with it, you will find that it is very flexible. It can be readily extended and the different sections are easily memorized, because they will remain constant. AX is always downstage right; CZ is always upstage left — unless the stage is particularly deep and the lighting designer is required to introduce a D row.

The common link is that A, B, and C always go across the stage, with A at the front; and X, Y, and Z run up stage, as shown in the diagram opposite.

Other methods of labeling will be found. Some are perfectly good; others are confusing, but none can be as flexible as this first method, once the main area is committed to memory.

Other methods are described on pages 78-79. These will need to be adapted if the stage is an unconventional shape.

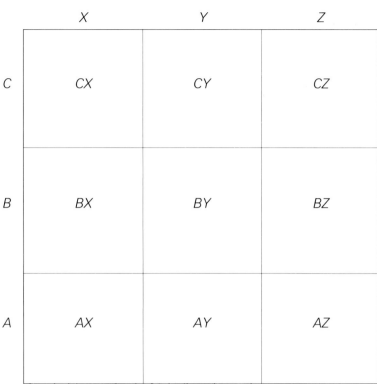

A suitable method of labeling the acting area

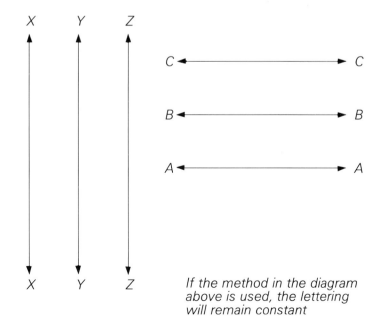

If the method in the diagram above is used, the lettering will remain constant

Labeling the acting area

1 *This method is most confusing of all as it adds yet another number on to the mark-up of a luminaire. Letters are far more readily recognized, amongst all the other numbers referring to color, circuit, and so on*

7	8	9
4	5	6
1	2	3

2 *This is better than method 1, although still very clumsy and rather time-consuming to write on each luminaire*

VII	VIII	IX
IV	V	VI
I	II	III

3 *This is the best of the alternatives but it lacks flexibility if the areas are to be memorized. (A need not always be downstage right nor H up center)*

G	H	I
D	E	F
A	B	C

4 *So this last system remains the best of all. For quick reference during rehearsal, when lighting the stage, or referring to a plan, this method is definitely the most useful, once one is familiar with its logic*

CX	CY	CZ
BX	BY	BZ
AX	AY	AZ

Labeling the acting area

For instance, imagine you are trying to take quick notes during a rehearsal. An actor walks across the stage in the down-stage position. One could write, "Henry V walks across down stage". But, if using method 4, the move is described as, "Henry V walks across A". So less time is required!

Even when the move is a more complicated one, this system simplifies matters. Here is another example: "Mr Waldo moves from up stage center to down stage center" or, "Mr Waldo moves through Y".

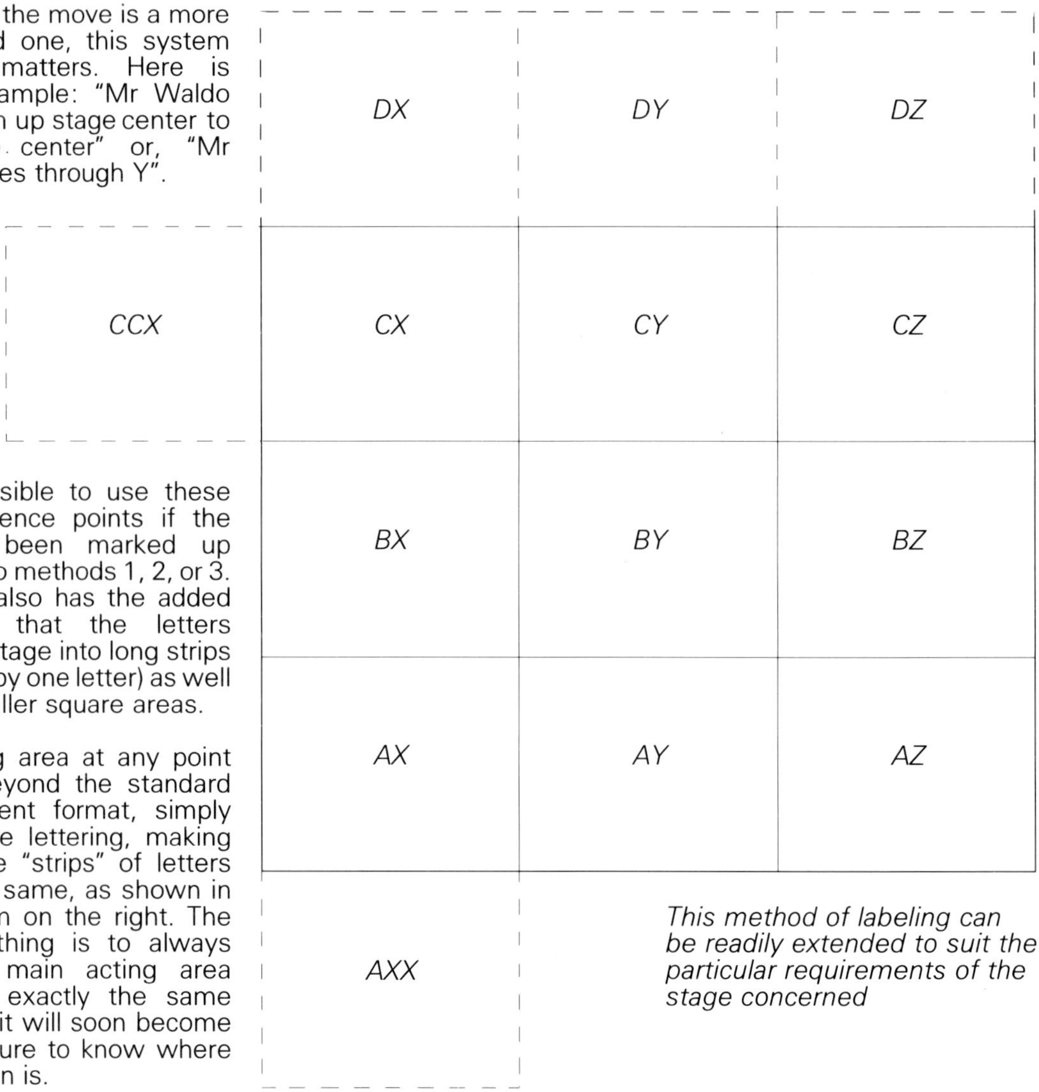

It is impossible to use these quick reference points if the plan has been marked up according to methods 1, 2, or 3. Method 4 also has the added advantage that the letters divide the stage into long strips (described by one letter) as well as into smaller square areas.

If an acting area at any point extends beyond the standard nine-segment format, simply add suitable lettering, making sure all the "strips" of letters remain the same, as shown in the diagram on the right. The important thing is to always keep the main acting area labeled in exactly the same way. Then it will soon become second nature to know where each section is.

	DX	DY	DZ
CCX	CX	CY	CZ
	BX	BY	BZ
	AX	AY	AZ
AXX			

This method of labeling can be readily extended to suit the particular requirements of the stage concerned

Lighting the stage sections

How to make up the lighting areas of a stage is very much up to the individual. Experiment with different ideas. A designer should ultimately choose the method that he or she finds most logical and easiest to use.

The most important point when dividing up an acting area is not to make each area so small that the rig becomes too complex. If this happens, merely providing cover for the acting area will exhaust the existing allocation of equipment. There will be no lights left for "specials", scenic effects, or whatever else might be required.

At the same time, the sections should never be too large. Otherwise there will not be enough controllable areas, and the cover from the luminaires lighting each section may be stretched too far.

For example, under normal circumstances, an acting area of twenty-four feet square can be divided into nine segments, each of which is eight feet square. Each of these nine segments is then lit like a little stage in itself.

Always start with the front light. It is this light that will largely light the actor so that he or she can be seen. If possible, each segment should be lit from both sides — at a 45 degree angle to the center, from the horizontal and vertical plane.

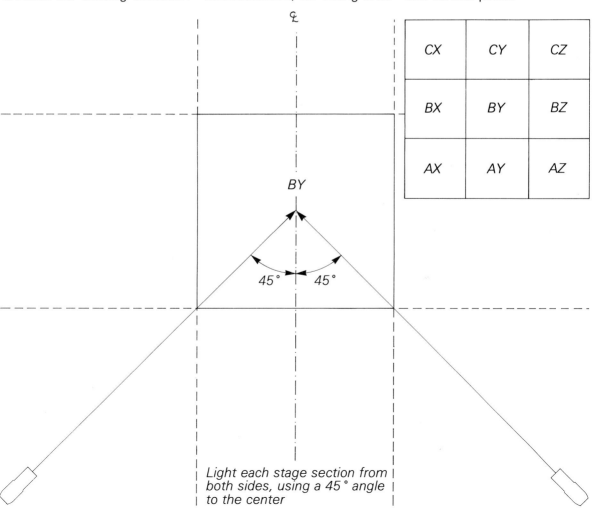

CX	CY	CZ
BX	BY	BZ
AX	AY	AZ

BY

45°   45°

Light each stage section from both sides, using a 45° angle to the center

Lighting the stage sections

So, however many segments the acting area has been divided into, each will have two luminaires for front lighting. On a nine-segment area, eighteen luminaires will be used. It is desirable (if space and budget allow) to double this allocation, so that each segment now has two luminaires per side. Thus four front luminaires will be used for each area. Two luminaires should be fitted with a cool tint and two with a warm tint. In this way, both a warm and cool wash can be used.

The temperature of the whole acting area can now be controlled (from warm to cool, or any state in between) by using both the color washes at varying light-intensity levels. This is obviously far more interesting and adaptable than flat white light.

So the whole acting area is lit, as shown in the small diagram below, by the overall effect of all these individual, controllable lighting areas.

If it is possible to fix each lamp to a different circuit, this effect may be clearly demonstrated. Each portion of the stage can be lit individually, or as a unit of the whole stage, to provide a good wash or cover of light.

The equipment used for this cover light will depend on the preference of the designer concerned — a choice that will be much easier to make after a careful study of all the available equipment (see pages 52-59).

When lighting through a proscenium arch, profiles are normally used to project the light through the proscenium arch opening. What happens next depends upon the design of the current production, but if side or back light is to be added at this point, then the supposed source of the light in the play must be considered.

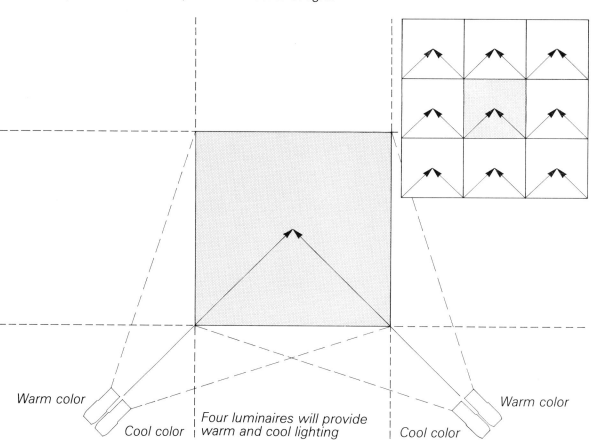

Warm color

Cool color

Four luminaires will provide warm and cool lighting

Warm color

Cool color

Key and fill light

Often the side or back light will provide the "key" light. The key light will be the strongest or most evident direction of light. It will emanate from the most natural point in that particular set — from the direction of whatever source of light is supposed to be there. This could be the moon, the sun, or a standard lamp!

Once the key light is decided upon, any other light on the set will be the fill light.

To further clarify the difference between key and fill light, let us take daylight as an example.

The sun is the light source, so the direction of this light will be the key light. However, we can still see an object or person facing away from the sun. This is possible because of the light which is dispersed or reflected. In a stage situation, this light which is reflected would be recognized as the fill light.

Reflected light may be transmitted from surrounding buildings, from objects, or bounced off the ground; dispersed light comes from the atmosphere and clouds.

So, for instance, try to visualize a box set with a window up stage and daylight outside. One would imagine the room to be lit by the light which is coming through the window.

WW→ Fill light (soft)
⟶ Key light (hard)

The sun is a source of key light, and reflected light acts as fill light

Key and fill light

The key light, therefore, will come from behind the actor (as though through the window). So, in this case, the back light will be the key light. As this is meant to be daylight, the designer ought to choose equipment which gives a strong hard light source for this back light; perhaps profiles or Pars.

The light bouncing off the room walls will be the fill light. The designer should therefore choose a soft light to use as side light, such as a Fresnel.

Obviously, if the room was lit by artificial light — perhaps by wall-lights set above the fireplace, the key light would then be from this source. So, in the set depicted in the diagram, the key light would be provided by the side light which crosses from stage left to stage right; and the fill light would be the light which crosses from stage right to stage left (as well as the back light and front light).

Specials

"Specials" may be added to the plan. A special is a lamp used outside the main acting area cover and which is there because it has a specific job to do. Perhaps, for instance, an actor needs to appear to be lit simply by the light of a candle.

Despite splitting the stage into numerous segments, it could be that each section is still too large and general to give the right effect. In this case, a lamp could be used, focused tightly on the area to be lit — just for that specific moment. This light would be called a special.

Hopefully by now it can be seen how the lighting plan may be constructed in an organized way, by working in stages so that nothing is forgotten. All the relevant parts of the stage will have been "covered" with whatever lighting structure has been chosen. It may be helpful to work through the plan in a logical way, as shown:

1 Front light
2 Key light
(side, back, or top light)
3 Fill light
(side, back, or top light)
4 Add specials
5 Add color
6 Draw on special effects
7 Circuit plan

However do not plan one element of the design in isolation. Always keep in mind the overall effect so that each

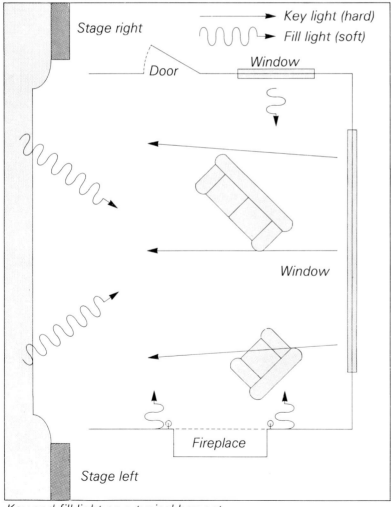

Key and fill light on a typical box set

element works with and complements the rest. Also do remember the scale of the operation, just what equipment and how much is available, how many circuits are available and even, in some cases, how much power. It is so frustrating to draw the ideal plan and then have to "butcher" it because there is more equipment on the plan than is actually available. As a rule, the plan is first drawn in pencil. A lot of paper planning is done long before the lighting designer can see a complete "run" of the show, (a rehearsal of the show from start to finish).

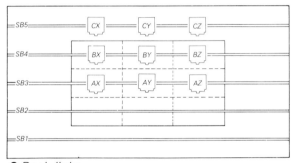

1 Front light

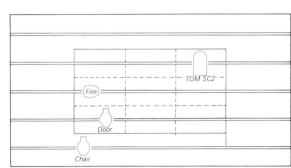

2 Side light

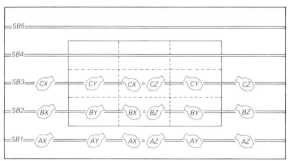

3 Back light

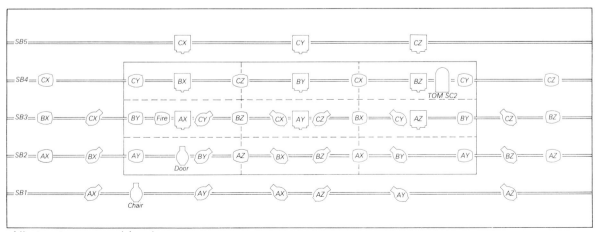

4 Specials

All structures combined

Final decisions

After seeing a "run", the lighting designer may wish to make some refinements to the lighting plan; perhaps adding or moving a few specials, or altering color to reflect a certain mood. When the last run is over, the lighting designer and director will meet once more and finalize the cueing notes. Only when the lighting designer is completely satisfied with the plan, will it be finalized and several duplicates made. It is worth remembering that many people will need a copy of the plan — the "riggers" and the electricians, the flyman (so the weight of each lighting bar can be assessed), the technical or stage director and, of course, a clean copy will also be needed for the lighting session — the moment of truth!

When all the luminaires have been allocated to the plan, each one must be clearly marked to indicate its type, its color reference number, its circuit

number, and its focus point. In the USA, an instrument and patch number would be shown.

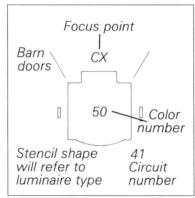

Marked-up luminaire

With experience the lighting designer will know, more or less, what a certain luminaire with a specific beam angle or angles will cover on stage; that is the amount of area it will light, given a specific throw distance. However there are times when even experienced designers

may find themselves relying on instinct or guesswork.

On such occasions it is best to do a quick calculation, to make sure the equipment used can cover the area required. For this, a plan and elevation of the rig will be needed. The beam angle of the luminaire in question and the distance of the luminaire from the area it is to light (the throw) must be known.

Then a simple line diagram, in the same scale as the plan and elevation, can be drawn and used to calculate the beam/ cover size. A protractor will be required. Use this to measure the angle required along the length of the throw.

The example here (drawn in a 1:25 scale) shows a 30 degree beam angle luminaire lighting a distance of 21.5 meters. It can be shown by the calculation that the amount of area covered by the light will be 1.27 meters.

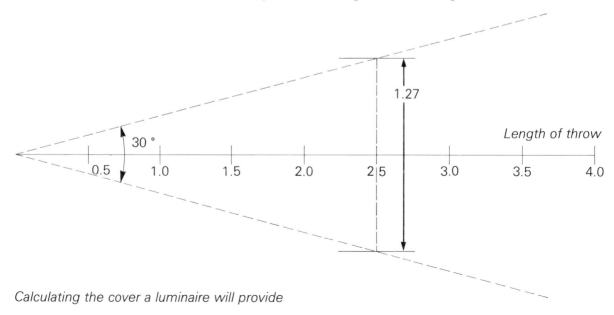

Calculating the cover a luminaire will provide

The thrust stage

So far, we have mainly considered the lighting of a proscenium stage, or at least a staging area where all the audience are sitting in front of the staging area. We should now take into account that not all productions and theaters are quite so conventional.

What considerations should be made when lighting the thrust stage, or for lighting a theater in the round (an arena stage), with an audience on all sides?

When a thrust stage is used, some of the audience will be viewing part of the staging area from the side. If the thrust stage is especially deep, the lighting designer should then consider whether the side of the thrust should be lit as though it were the front — or in the same way as the "real" front. Thus it could be said that a thrust stage has three fronts!

If this option is chosen, the side light for this area will also act as front light for some of the audience, and so this must be taken into account. Most certainly, in these cases, side light is essential to allow actors to be seen when facing stage left or right.

It may be argued that lights should be placed at a 45 degree angle to frontlight the side of a thrust stage. However, the problem is that this light would then interfere with the back light (as shown in diagram A).

Instead, it is best to use a flat front light which comes straight in from the horizontal plane to the side of the thrust stage. This is quite adequate and, in most cases, will look rather better anyway.

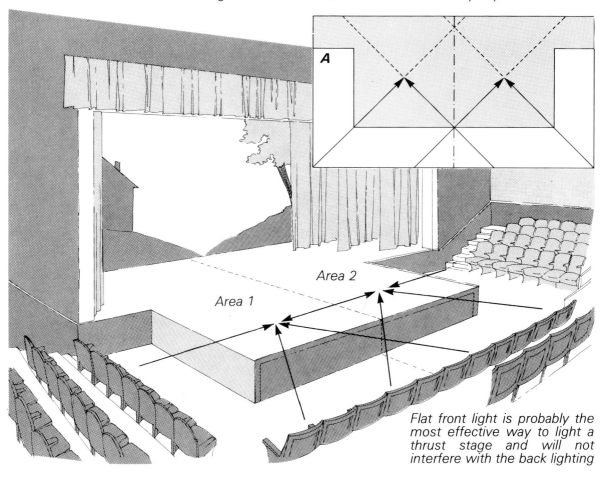

Flat front light is probably the most effective way to light a thrust stage and will not interfere with the back lighting

Lighting in the round (arena stage)

When lighting a theater in the round, it must be remembered that some lighting structures previously dealt with no longer exist in a normal form. This is due to the fact that there is now an audience on every side, 360 degrees around the stage.

The structures therefore take on a different form, depending on where one is sitting around the stage. These changes affect front light, side light, cross light, back light, and silhouette — this last being almost impossible.

It can be seen from the diagram that the people sitting in block A will interpret the lighting structures quite differently to those sitting in blocks B, C, and D. The audience in each block of seats sees the lighting from a different angle.

Take, for example one light source coming into the stage from the front (on the plan).

For those people sitting in block A, this light source is front light; for those in B and D, however, the light becomes side light; while for those in block C, the same light source becomes back light. So, in theater in the round, the creation of good acting-area cover means that the front, side, and back light become as one unit — the apparent structure of which will depend totally on the angle from which it is viewed.

When lighting in the round, the initial approach to the provision of acting-area cover is much the same as for a conventional stage. The stage must first be split into areas.

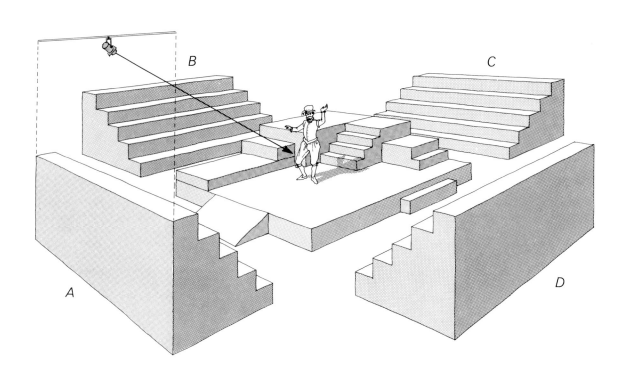

The audience in each block of seats will see the lighting from a different angle

The most obvious way of lighting each area would be to hang each luminaire at a 45 degree angle to each of the four viewing "fronts", as shown in the first diagram below.

Lighting all nine segments like this would indeed give an excellent acting-area cover. By doubling the luminaires for each area (using two for each lighting position), a warm and a cool wash could be provided, as described earlier.

However, this method is obviously a rather extravagant one and may quickly consume all the allocation of equipment. Eight luminaires will be needed for each area so nine segments require seventy-two luminaires.

If equipment budgeting renders this method impracticable, use a wider-angled separation of the lights, setting them 120 degrees apart. In this way, three luminaires instead of four may be used to light each segment. If doubling up is required, six luminaires will be sufficient, and fifty-four would cover all nine segments of the stage.

This second method reduces The number of luminaires needed to provide the acting-area cover and yet still provides a perfectly adequate and adaptable lighting system.

If coloring the stage is required, but it is not desirable to dramatically color the actor's face, then top light must be considered. This is one of the few lighting structures that will remain constant from whichever point the stage is viewed. To make top light available in each segment would be ideal, and greatly enhance all the sculpturing qualities of the design.

If possible, when a designer is lighting a show, he or she should arrange to see a "run" from each viewing point. This will ensure that, when lighting from any chosen point, the light from the opposite side has not been overlooked.

It may, in fact, be advisable to pair up opposite luminaires. Then, when called upon to light an area from one side, the complimentary luminaire on the

opposite side, which is to cover the same area, is automatically illuminated.

Hopefully this literally "new angle" on stage lighting will work well and the challenge of different surroundings will teach all those involved, including the lighting designer, a great deal. He or she may well collect a few new and useful ideas that can be applied to the conventional stage. It is all too easy to become stale if every play is undemanding.

In any event, whatever the shape of the stage or wherever the audience sit, the lighting designer should always try to remember the objectives — that is to reveal the actors, using the lights on the stage to create a temporary world around them. Whether it is moonlight slanting in through an attic window, midday in the Sahara desert, or "special" Christmas-tree lights on a darkened stage, the lighting should be a vital link between the actors, the environment created around them, and the audience who have come to watch.

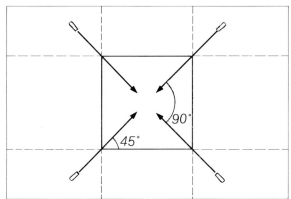

Lighting for a single segment using a 90 degree separation

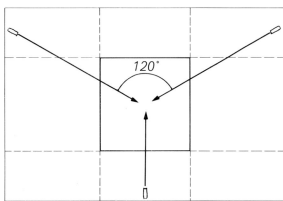

Lighting for a single segment using a 120 degree separation

Production procedure

At this stage of a production, good organization is the most important element. It is now that the designer will reap the benefits of a well-planned and fully prepared lighting scheme. At last all the ideas will come to fruition — but this will be achieved only if preceded by thorough ground work.

This procedure is analyzed mainly from the mechanical point of view, especially in its initial stages, as it is most important to understand the technicalities involved.

Once the lighting rig is safely in position and every luminaire is correctly angled, then the focusing can begin. At this point, the designer will be busy directing operations, and will continue to do so through the lighting session and rehearsals.

When the final dress rehearsal comes to an end, the task of the lighting designer will be largely over until the next show. (This does not apply, of course, to the lighting designer of a small company who is also the operator during a performance.) Lighting may need to be changed occasionally during production; the timing of the play may alter, or the director might decide to change some part of it. Luminaires may move slightly or need readjustment.

Generally though, apart from perhaps the supervision of the rig's removal, the designer can switch attention to the next production or to whatever else is "in the pipeline".

During the production schedule, the lighting will gradually have evolved and taken shape. The symbols on the plan will have been replaced by luminaires, and the ideas in the lighting designer's mind will, hopefully, have been realized on the stage. The whole production team will have been working very hard at this stage, in order to see the final culmination of their efforts. If all this has been achieved with co-operation and mutual understanding, they will all enjoy a well-deserved glow of success when they finally see their particular talents blended together into live theater.

Pre-planning

The lighting plan (lighting plot)

The completed lighting plan is the lighting designer's main means of communication at this stage. It is through this plan that all the lighting requirements are made known to the rest of the production team. (Exactly how to compile one is described on pages 72-3.)

Make sure the plan has properly covered every necessary detail; then have sufficient copies of this duplicated to enable every member of the electrics team to have one each. The other production departments will also require a copy and one must be made available for the lighting session. Make sure that these are all distributed in good time (but not so early that they can be forgotten or mislaid!)

Color

If new color filters are needed, purchase these well in advance of the "fit-up". In this way, if there are any problems in obtaining the particular type required, there will still be plenty of time to find an alternative or a different source.

If the budget allows, buy more than just the minimum number required; then you will not be compromised during the fit-up, if it turns out that more gels are required than anticipated.

Look at the lighting plan and draw up a list of the colors that will need to be cut to luminaire size. These can be classified under luminaire size, or according to the position for which they are intended. The second method is probably the best because it is easier to find the necessary piece when that particular part of the rig is being constructed.

Store all the required colors in a separate envelope for each location. Clearly label every envelope and then there will be no frantic searching later.

Hire of equipment

Any equipment to be hired must be ordered in good time and then carefully checked when it arrives. Make sure it is all in perfect working order and is exactly what is needed. Some pieces of equipment must have special cable so, if this is the case, do check that this has been supplied too and meets your requirements.

Most rental companies enclose a spare lamp with their equipment. Ensure that this is sound — and if it does have to be used during the course of the production, remember to keep the "blown" lamp in a safe place. This will act as proof that this has actually happened. Failure to produce the old lamp could result in an unwelcome extra bill for its replacement.

Cables and adapters

Study the plan once again — this time to count the number of times that pairing occurs.(This is when more than one luminaire is using a single dimmer, as described on page 147.)

Ensure that there are enough adapters ("two-fers") available for all the pairing to be done and that there is enough cable available to feed each luminaire. Always check you are using the correct size cable for the load. This is particularly important when the venue is previously unknown to you. If working in a foreign country, all the electrical equipment will have to come under close scrutiny to make sure local regulations are complied with and safety standards are met.

Fuses and spare lamps

During the fit-up and the subsequent removal of the rig (derig), the luminaires will have to be moved about so they are more liable to damage than at any other time. Handle them as carefully as possible. This is the most likely time for lamps to "blow", especially if the electricians are at all rough with the luminaires. It is therefore wise to keep a stock of lamps and fuses in case they are ever needed.

The electrical team

The electricians and riggers will be working very hard to rig the lighting in the time allowed, usually under quite difficult circumstances.

In professional theater, the management cannot allow much time between shows because money is lost when the theater is closed. So the quicker the better!

In amateur productions the pressure may not be so great if the company own their own theater, but often as not, the hall is used by other groups or societies and it may not be available until the very last minute. Neither professional nor amateur can afford to book an empty theater for too long.

This means that time is very precious. Not only will the lighting crew be working against the clock, but the set too will probably have to be constructed and completed in a short space of time. Stage management, carpenters, and the props department will all be busy. The actors, as well, will want to use this opportunity to rehearse in the new environment — so there is often competition for stage space and an over-riding sense of panic!

Much depends on how well organized the production is as a whole. It is up to the lighting designer to ensure that his or her particular department is in order. If everything has been carefully planned, then the electricians will know exactly what is expected of them and, despite probably having to work long hours, will be prepared to "pull their weight" — provided they are confident that there is method in the madness and that their needs have been considered.

It may be a good idea to work out a timetable beforehand. Analyze the lighting plan and write down just what has to be accomplished in the time available. Try to be realistic in the allotment of time and remember to allow for a few well-earned tea-breaks!

Do not try to win the co-operation of the electrical team with large quantities of alcohol as there will probably be some ladder climbing ahead!

If the fit-up is going to involve a good deal of ladder work, it is best to have a minimum of three people on the team. One person will climb the ladder, another holds it steady, and the third will be able to pass up the luminaires as required.

Focusing is best done by a team of four. Once again, the first person (who will need to have two strong arms and a head for heights) scales the ladder, ready to focus the luminaires. The second person steadies the ladder, the third puts the circuits up on the lighting board, and the lighting designer must direct the proceedings to make sure the focusing is accurate.

It is important to allow sufficient time to focus correctly. Any mistakes made at this session will have to be rectified later and may well add to the frustrations of a future lighting session or rehearsal. Allow an average of three minutes per luminaire.

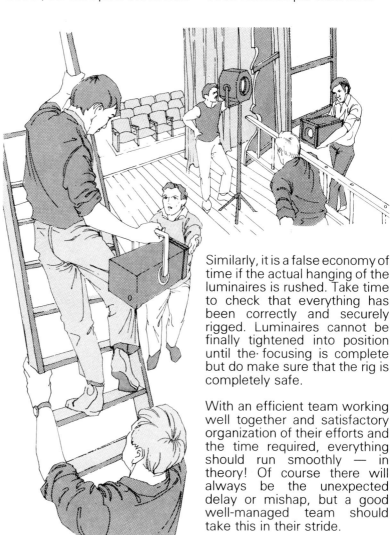

Similarly, it is a false economy of time if the actual hanging of the luminaires is rushed. Take time to check that everything has been correctly and securely rigged. Luminaires cannot be finally tightened into position until the focusing is complete but do make sure that the rig is completely safe.

With an efficient team working well together and satisfactory organization of their efforts and the time required, everything should run smoothly — in theory! Of course there will always be the unexpected delay or mishap, but a good well-managed team should take this in their stride.

The fit-up

Safety

There are invariably other people working on the stage simultaneously with the lighting team. It is sensible therefore to ensure that your work does not impede that of others. Hopefully they will respond by showing some consideration for your needs. Of course this is not always the case and, if another group of people are less well organized, this may lead to short tempers and short cuts. The theater at this time has all the dangers of a building site and great care must be taken to avoid accidents.

This is especially important when scenery is in transit and if there are counterweighted flying bars (or pipes) being rigged. It is vital to be aware of people working above, and below. It is always possible that a heavy object could be dropped. A shout of, "Heads!" is pointless if there is no reaction from the people below.

The safety of the mechanical and electrical equipment is always important. Check and double-check every fitting. Make sure all the nuts are adequately tightened. Don't leave equipment lying around. Make sure plugs are wired correctly and properly inserted into their sockets. Any loose cable must be securely taped to the bars. If any ropes are used, make sure these are sound and are safely anchored. Don't balance ladders on uneven floors. Be especially cautious if the rig is a particularly high one. Scaffolding, or a Tallescope, may have to be used, or even, in extreme situations, a "bosun's chair". Any such operation

A Tallescope

requires a particular awareness of the inherent dangers.

In any event, great care and discipline must be exercised throughout this stage of the production.

Removing the rig

Occasionally an existing rig may bear a close resemblance to the design of the new rig about to be put into operation. In this

case, it will obviously be in your interests to adjust it accordingly rather than to totally dismantle it. In normal circumstances, however, if a rig is still in position from the previous production, it will be necessary to remove this, and start afresh.

Begin by unplugging all the cables from the dimmers. Then unplug and remove them from the lighting bar (or batten). Carefully coil and tape cables.

Never try to coil the cable between your elbow and your hand as this twists the wire cores and will strain them unnecessarily. Instead it is best to coil the cable by holding it just behind the plug or socket in one hand, and then use the other hand to make large loops (about one meter). Twist the cable as you do this so that it hangs properly without any kinks in it. Once the cable has been carefully coiled, it can then be taped at one end to keep it neatly in shape.

The next job is to remove all the luminaires' color frames. When this has been done, close all the barn doors and shutters to prevent their being damaged.

If the rig is on a flying system, the counterweights must all be unloaded before any luminaires are removed from the bar. To remove any equipment at all from a fully counterweighted bar could be very dangerous. Counterweights are extremely heavy and their sheer weight could cause the bar to fly out, risking life and limb, and possibly damaging the building. Should an electrician be foolish enough to start work on a counterweighted bar, there is every chance of flying out with it and adding to the spectacle! Never ever take this risk.

Once the weights have been unloaded, then the luminaires can be safely removed and the next lighting bar derigged.

If the rig is on fixed bars, then it may be necessary to use a Tallescope or a rung ladder, remembering to take all the necessary precautions. It is sometimes very useful to use a rope carefully hung over the lighting bar (or pipe) so that the luminaires can be gently lowered to the person waiting down below.

Once all the previous rig has been carefully removed and unwanted equipment carefully stored away, then the new fit-up can begin in earnest.

Rigging

One lighting bar will have to be rigged at a time. Having worked out in what order the hanging should be done (perhaps to fit in with the set construction), next gather all the necessary equipment together and keep it in a convenient place. Make sure everything that you need is ready before you start.

Place the first luminaire on the lighting bar as indicated on the lighting plan. Angle it so it is pointing in approximately the right direction. Although this is only a rough position, it will help, at a later stage, to speed up the focusing session. Tighten the hook clamp and attach the safety chain to the bar, leaving sufficient "slack" to allow movement of the luminaire to any angle.

Continue to rig all the other luminaires on to the bar, making sure that each one has sufficient space around it. The luminaires must be able to be adjusted during the focusing session without "fouling" each other. Provided the plan has been drawn up properly to scale, there should be no such problems to contend with.

Continue in this way on the next bar. A methodical "plan of campaign" will reap dividends at this time.

Once all the luminaires have been rigged up according to the lighting plan, make sure all the necessary colors and accessories have been fitted and that every luminaire has been allocated a lamp!

Spot bars (or pipes)

If an internally-wired spot bar is to be used, start plugging the luminaires into this. Always begin plugging in at the opposite end of the bar to the cable or "tripe" feed. In this way, should any extra "ways" have to be inserted later, then shorter cable lengths can be used. There will be no need for cable to travel the full length of the bar to reach each luminaire.

Tie the socket of the extension cable around the bar, next to the luminaire it is feeding. Then tape it along the bar at intervals so it remains neatly in place.

Keep "luminaire tail" loose so that the luminaire can move without pulling on the cable. Where a cable leaves the end of a spot bar, tape it to the end of this to avoid placing any strain on the plugs and sockets.

Label and check

The next step in the rigging session is to make sure that everything is clearly labeled and working properly. It is important to do this efficiently, both for safety reasons and to ensure a smooth-running production schedule. First "flash" through the rigged bar to test the offstage ends of the feed cables and mark them with the circuit number. Then label the plugs coming off the spot bar with their correct circuit numbers.

At the same time, check that everything is working properly. Each plug must be inserted into a working socket. Do this one plug at a time, and as each luminaire is lit, check it against the lighting plan and write the circuit number clearly on the plug top. Use large lettering on adhesive tape so it can be easily seen, even in the dark.

If any luminaire fails to light, first unplug it and then make a visual check to see if the lamp's filament is still intact. If the lamp has blown, simply replace it. Should the lamp appear to be in working order, try plugging the luminaire into another cable and working socket. If it now proves operational, this means the cable may be faulty or there is a loose connection in the plug or the socket.

Try to correct all such faults well ahead of the focusing session. It is far easier to be able to work through the problems now, when they can be dealt with at ground level, than to be struggling up ladders later when everything is in its final position. Never work on any equipment that is still plugged in.

Focusing

Once all the lighting bars have been rigged and checked, and when everything has been labeled, the bars can then be plugged into their circuits.

To complete the operation, make a final check through all the rig, circuit by circuit, using the lighting board. Double-check that all the plugging and colors used are correct and that every piece of equipment is in working order.

It may not be possible to rig every single piece of equipment at this stage if the set is still under construction.

Some side lighting (such as booms or tormentors) and practical lamps on the stage set itself, or lights that are actually attached to scenery, may have to wait until slightly later. If this is the case, make sure that all the necessary equipment is prepared and fully organized.

Exercise the same methodical check and double-check when their rigging is finally finished, and do not be hustled into overlooking any aspect of this important operation.

Thus, rigging a normal lighting bar may be undertaken safely and successfully if the following routine is carefully observed:

1. Postion the luminaires on the bar, remembering to tighten the hook clamps and to fix the safety chains.

2. Plug luminaires to internally-wired spot bars and to all the extension cables.

3. Open all shutters, barn doors, and color luminaires.

4. "Flash" through the tripe ends and mark all plugs with their correct circuit numbers.

5. Plug the marked tripe ends into the circuit board or patch panel as appropriate.

Focusing

Focusing is, perhaps, the most important part of production procedure.

Each part is, of course, a vital element in its own right and must be executed efficiently, but to achieve really good lighting, and fulfil the realization of the lighting designer's perception of the play, a successful focusing session is absolutely essential.

Ideally, four people will be needed to focus quickly and safely. The lighting designer will stay at stage-floor level and give the directions from there. The electricican will focus the luminaires, according to these directions, from his or her position at the top of the ladder. The third person will be the control-board operator who brings up the circuits; and the fourth person is the one who foots the bottom of the ladder.

There are two ways to focus. The first possible method is to stand with one's back to the luminaire concerned, in order to avoid being blinded by the light. Then direct the electrician to center the luminaire on to the back of your head and judge its position by the effect of the heat on the back of the neck. This is not altogether satisfactory as it is difficult to be accurate without actually looking at the equipment being adjusted.

The second (and rather more efficient) method is to adjust the luminaire's light intensity to a low level so that it can be looked at comfortably. It is much easier to center the luminaire now as you can see the position of the filament in relation to the reflector. Once the luminaire has been centered to your satisfaction, the light can be brought up to full and its effect on the scenery, and so on, properly ascertained.

As each luminaire is focused, make sure that it is able to provide sufficient cover for the particular area that it has been allocated — check that every part of it is lit. If the area concerned is an acting area, ensure that the light overlaps the divisions slightly. Then the actors will be lit completely evenly as they cross from one area to another. Test this by walking around the appropriate parts of the stage with the relevant luminaires lit as they will be during the play.

Remember throughout all this the actors' actual positions on the stage. They may be lying down or sitting on a low chair and this must be considered.

If a beam hits part of the scenery, try to disguise the edges of the beam by softening them slightly or aiming them towards the tops of doorways, picture rails, or whatever part of the set is convenient! Be careful, also, to avoid unwanted shadows or hot spots. Off-stage luminaires (or those set behind a backing) might cause problems in this way, especially when an actor is waiting in the wings. Try to visualize just exactly where everyone will be.

Another problem that might need attention is spill or ghost light. As each luminaire is focused and set, do check thoroughly that no unwanted leakage of light appears on the proscenium or any borders, scenery, or backcloth. Have a quick glance around the whole set before you move on to the next light. It is so much simpler to eradicate at this stage than when several luminaires are working together and the "guilty party" is not quite so easily recognized.

The focusing team

Throughout the operation, the four members of the lighting team who are working together have their separate but co-ordinated roles to play.

The lighting designer

The lighting designer carries the ultimate responsibility for the overall success of the focusing session. Speed is usually essential but accuracy is equally important. Every luminaire must be literally "spot on"! A few inches difference really does matter, so do check every luminaire properly.

Remember that the lamps heat up very quickly, so don't call up a luminaire until the electrician is ready for it. Then stand in the center of area to be lit and use one of the methods already described to center the luminaire to head height.

Once this has been achieved, step out of the beam and adjust the size to cover the appropriate area. Check that this has been completely lit by walking the area. Finally, adjust the barn

doors and shutters to remove unwanted light, and double-check that everything is in order. Carry in your mind clearly the exact function of each luminaire and make sure this is properly achieved.

The electrician

The electrician must first ensure that he or she is in a safe and comfortable position and that all the luminaires are within reach. The next step is to check that all the shutters and barn doors are open and that any Fresnel luminaires are adjusted so that their beams are "spotted down" to the smallest possible beam angle. This will make it easier to center them properly. Make sure that all necessary tools are readily to hand.

Once this has all been done, the electrician should inform the lighting designer that focusing can begin. The designer will then call up the circuit and give instructions as the focusing proceeds. The electrician must follow directions and, as each angle is finalized, lock it into position and tighten all the nuts.

The electrician will be able to see the stage well from the top of the ladder and perhaps is better placed than the rest of the team to check exactly what the light beam is doing. Therefore it can often be helpful to the lighting designer if the electrician makes sure that, from his or her viewpoint too, there are no apparent problems.

Before leaving one focused luminaire for another, double-check that it is securely locked off and will not slide out of position at a later stage.

The speed and efficiency of the operation largely depends on the quality of the electrician!

The board operator

The board operator is the one who is most familiar with all the controls, especially if the board is a very complicated one. He or she is also the most remote member of the team, probably being at some distance from the core of activity but, like the electrician, it will be necessary to follow instructions promptly and to co-ordinate with the rest of the team. Communications between them all may range from shouting, and using a system of signals, to an intercom arrangement. Check that any intercom or telephone system is working properly before focusing begins.

Unless the lighting designer gives instructions otherwise, it is usual to bring up just one circuit at a time. So, when a circuit is requested, put it into effect; then remove any other circuits already being tested.

The ladder crew

The ladder crew, albeit often only one person, must always see that the safety of the operation is ensured. The ladder must be held firmly and then moved as required. Again, it is imperative that all instructions are followed precisely.

The lighting rehearsal

The aim of this first lighting session is to see for the first time on stage an idea of how all the lighting will look, cue by cue. It will not yet be perfect — this first session will be more like a

Rehearsals

rough sketch than a detailed drawing, but, if the focusing has been carefully executed, the desired effects should all be there, ready to be molded into their final form when set and actors have all been absorbed into the pattern.

With the focusing complete and the rig all ready, the lighting designer should also be fully prepared for this session.

It is best to view the lighting from a position about halfway down the auditorium. This will usually ensure a balanced lighting state, neither too dark from the back of the auditorium nor too bright near to the stage. (It will be necessary at later rehearsals to check the lighting from other positions, to see that it is correct from every seat in the house.)

Having chosen a good site, ensure that you have everything you need ready, preferably on a desk or table so that script, plots, and the lighting plan can be spread out before you. Do make certain it is possible to communicate with everyone concerned from this vantage point, most especially with the electricians.

A low-level light may be a useful addition to the paraphernalia now doubtless littering an already crowded desk.

A "walker" will need to move about on the stage, aping the actors, to enable the effects of the lighting to be judged effectively. Make sure that someone is ready to take on this task. To light the actors so they can be seen is the prime object of the exercise and this cannot

be assessed on an empty stage. When everything the designer needs is ready and all the lighting team have announced that they, also, are fully organized, the lighting session can begin.

It is best to commence with the house in darkness (allowing for any exit lights or orchestra cover), and then to gradually introduce the required lighting composition for each cue. Begin with the main light source or the key light. For instance, light emanating from a window or doorway, or the daylight slowly filling a cyclorama, should be brought up to its required level before the overall cover lighting is introduced.

It is normal practice to begin at the beginning and then to follow the cue synopsis through to the end. This allows everyone to see the lighting patterns as part of the overall scheme and to evaluate their effects within the context of the whole.

However, this means that if there are any doubts about a particular piece of equipment or effect, it will be necessary to check this beforehand. In fact, a quick test of every circuit before the session begins in earnest may eliminate any later irritating interruptions to the run-through.

As each lighting state is composed on the stage and evaluated with the assistance of the "walker", it must be labeled with a cue number. If both lighting designer and director are happy with the result, it can then be plotted on the lighting board. Never rush this stage. Careful plotting of circuits is vital. A mistake now

could alter the intended effect of the lighting, or even totally ruin a composition.

It is often wise not to take the lighting circuits up to full at this initial stage, even for a very sunny scene. The director may well ask for more light and it is most frustrating if you have already exhausted all your reserves. Always keep a little extra light "in stock", just in case this happens!

Light levels will be adjusted within each composition until the overall picture suits all concerned. Make sure that the colors which have been chosen blend together well and that any changes are not too abrupt or unnatural.

Always allow the electrician or operator sufficient time to plot everything properly and clearly. If a memory board is being used (see pages 40-41), then all this will be far less tedious and time-consuming.

During this lighting rehearsal, the members of the production team will all have their comments to make, according to their particular interest in the show. These must be taken into account when possible.

A lighting designer should aim to achieve his or her vision of the play, but not at the expense of set or costumes. The director will have the last word if there are any difficulties about this.

Hopefully, if the pre-planning stages have been thoroughly exploited and comprehensive discussion has already taken place, there will be no such clash of interests.

A good well-organized lighting department will be appreciated by the rest of the production personnel and the arduous lighting session may well turn out to be a successful culmination of earlier efforts.

The technical rehearsal

The technical rehearsal brings together, for the first time, the actors and the technical aspects of the show. This will include lighting, sound, and scene changes. (In some instances, an initial technical rehearsal may be held without any actors present at all.) The purpose of this rehearsal is to eliminate the inevitable difficulties that result when all the different departments are finally brought together.

During this rehearsal it is at last possible to see how all the lighting cues fit into the play as a whole and how they co-ordinate with whatever else is going on. A particularly difficult lighting sequence may have to be run through several times to ensure that it can be correctly handled and that the effect is exactly what is required.

Should any luminaires have to be moved between scenes, then this is the time to ensure that everyone knows what is required of them and that there is sufficient time available to effect such a change.

The first technical rehearsal will expose any discrepancies in the production. It is all too easy to overlook some small detail, hitherto masked by the fact that every department has been operating fairly independently up until now.

This is the time to iron out any such problem, as amicably as possible, for by now nerves and tiredness are probably beginning to take their toll.

During the technical rehearsal, lighting states can be modified by the lighting designer as necessary. Do remember that the board operator will be very busy, especially if the board is a manual one, and do not make impossible demands of his or her time and patience.

The dress rehearsal

Every production is different. The one thing they all have in common is that any dress rehearsal should always be approached as though it is an actual performance. There may indeed be several dress rehearsals prior to the actual first night, but each one should be regarded as "the real thing" so that the timing of the production and all its potential problems can be properly and accurately assessed.

It is only if this approach is taken, that the technical departments can be confident about their cues. For instance, the operator of a manual board needs to be sure that a tricky lighting sequence is actually possible in the time allowed; and it is only thus that the designer can be sure that a lighting cue is being taken at the optimum moment. It may be that adjustments will have to be made. If lighting levels are obviously wrong, try to make any changes gradually so that the acting company are not suddenly startled by a flood of light or unexpectedly plunged into darkness.

The timing of a particular sequence may have altered dramatically due to some extra "business" the actors have introduced, or because of an awkward scene or costume change. Many minor problems arise that have not been considered before, and after this rehearsal the director may be justified in asking for a particular sequence to be re-run in order to make any adjustments and ensure that the scene will run smoothly.

Throughout, the lighting designer must take this last opportunity to study the effects of the lighting from as many different parts of the theater as possible, until he or she is convinced that every member of the audience will see just what was intended. This is particularly important with theater in the round (arena).

At last the final dress rehearsal is over. The culmination of many weeks of planning and preparation await the response of the audience. The lighting designer will have studied in detail so much that is simply taken for granted by an audience when they see a well-organized production.

A smooth and enjoyable production is only possible if the lighting has been well planned and organized. With each step, from script to lighting plan, to rigging, focusing, and rehearsal, each part of the procedure lays the foundation for the next, and must be done carefully and efficiently if the whole structure is to remain stable. Good ground work is essential if the lighting is to succeed.

Color

Using color carefully

The impact of color on a stage is always one of the most important factors. The effect of lighting with color can be particularly dramatic. If it is overdone, the result may even be catastrophic!

The way in which a lighting designer interprets color can "make or break" every aspect of a show's design concept. All the visual elements of the production can be affected by a single wash of color.

No matter what has been achieved with set or costume colors, the lighting designer can alter the end result. Sometimes, for certain scenes, it may in fact, need to be changed but in general, great care must be taken not to use lighting color effects indiscriminately.

Under normal circumstances, the color of illumination should enhance both the set and the costumes, and not fight against them. Add to this the need to use color to create atmosphere, mood, and the time of day or year; or to give the appearance that the scene is lit by, perhaps, candles or firelight — and it can be seen that this is one of the most demanding and exciting areas of stage lighting.

*Ring Round the Moon
at the Bristol Old Vic*

Color theory

Color effects for different types of shows will usually call for quite different techniques. The lighting for a variety show or a musical, for instance, would not use color in the same way as it would be used in a box set for an Alan Ayckbourn comedy.

The first two shows might well make lavish use of color, with many changes, whereas a straight play would use more subdued, natural color, of which the audience would scarcely be conscious.

Here we can deal only with the main principles of color. The final selection of what to use depends on the type of production and is very much a matter of personal choice for the lighting designer at the time.

Primary colors

A lighting designer has, as tools for the work ahead, three colors from which all other colors in light are made. These are the primaries of red, blue, and green. Together, they make white light; they are derived from white light; and various mixtures of them will create all other known colors.

Color mixing

To demonstrate what color mixing can achieve, set up a simple experiment. Take three profile spotlights of the same type and focus them to create three, overlapping hard-edged beams, as shown on the right.

So now there are three circles of white light. Add one primary color filter to each of the lights, and where all three overlap a fairly good white light is formed.

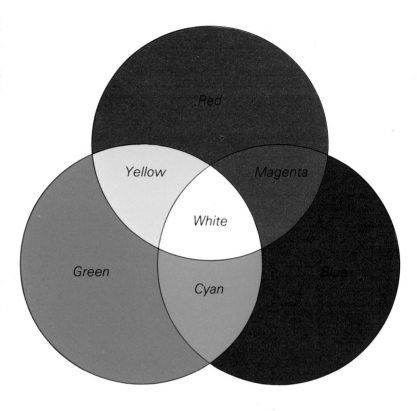

The other overlapping effects are as follows:

Green over red = yellow
Green over blue = cyan
Blue over red = magenta

Quite simply, the eye has three color receptors, — one for each of the primary colors just discussed — red, green, and blue. So any form of these colors, in any combination, can be seen by the eye. If it were possible for a color to exist without the properties of red, green, and blue, the eye would simply not see it.

It follows that if mixing the three primaries gives white light, then splitting white light should produce every different color; from the red (long wave), through green (medium wave), to blue (short wave).

Indeed it was Newton who first demonstrated this by splitting white light through a prism. In 1704 Newton wrote, "Every body reflects the rays of its own color more copiously than the rest, and from their excess and predominance in the reflected light, has its color". So every object actually reflects many wavelengths of light.

The longer the wavelength, the redder the object; the shorter the wavelength, the bluer the object, while green objects reflect the medium wavelength.

Why, therefore, do we not have a rig with three lights focused into the same area, and each light fitted with a different primary color gel? Theoretically, by mixing these primaries and altering the proportions of each (by using different light levels), we should then be able to achieve any color required.

Unfortunately, in practice this method does not work very well. There are several reasons.

Most importantly, the primary gels available are close — but not true — primaries. The blue is a deeper color than the others and lets less light through it, so there is an imbalance of light output. Also, as the level of the light is dimmed, the lamp will tend to glow towards yellow, especially at very low level.

Thus the end result is a very off-white light source being projected through a colored filter which is not a true primary.

Because of these various imperfections, an exact color reproduction will not be achieved. Only true primary reproduction at every level will produce a perfect "spectrum" color reproduction.

However, if the shades of color required are not too critical, the three-color primary mixing does work to a certain extent.

It is quite feasible to use a three-color batten which contains each primary in order to produce interesting colors on a white cloth or cyclorama. It is also possible to use all the three primaries together to make an acceptable white.

Lighting the acting area

It is generally true that when lighting an acting area, rather lighter and more subtle tints are used to color skin tones — not the heavy colors produced by a simple primary mix, such as the one just described.

Strong coloring of the stage is best left to the back light as this will not affect an actor's face. Use this lighting structure, and then the general appearance of the stage can be made to look bright blue without the actors having to sport bright-blue faces as well!

The choice of tint or color used obviously depends on the type of illumination required — day, night, interior, exterior, or whatever the play demands.

To give some indication of the degree of color to use in normal frontlight conditions, here are a few examples which have been selected from the Lee range of colors:

Notice that "No color" or "Open white" can be categorized as a warm color. This is particularly true when used at low light levels. The range of color from a "white" light at level one to white light at full is quite astonishing.

All of these colors are most useful as "tints". They make excellent skin-tone colors because they do not color the skin so unnaturally as to make the actor look like a witch or a demon. Yet, at the same time, they will add to the general feel or mood of the scene.

Warms	Cinemoid		Lee	
Straws	73	Straws	159	No color straw
	3	Straw tint	103	Straw
Yellows/	50	Pale yellow	212	LCT yellow
ambers	47	Apricot	147	Apricot
Pinks	51	Gold tint	151	Gold tint
	62	Pale gold	152	Pale gold
	53	Pale salmon	153	Pale salmon
	54	Pale rose	154	Pale rose
	7A	Light rose	107	Light rose
	9	Light salmon	109	Light salmon
No color		Open white		
Cools				
Blues	17	Steel tint	117	Steel blue
	40	Pale blue	144	No color blue
	45	Daylight blue	201-3	Tungstun to daylight
	61	Slate blue	161	Slate blue
	67	Steel blue		No substitute
	69	Ariel blue		No substitute

Color practice

Color correction

If white light is desired by the designer, it may seem an easy operation — simply do not put any color in the lamp. However, if the designer then uses that light at a low level, anything but white light will be produced. Instead, the stage will be filled with a yellowish murk.

Fortunately, there are gels on the market whose main purpose in life is to "color correct". Such gels can be found in the Lee Colour range. There are four gels, in various grades of blue, all of which can remove the creaminess of low-level white light.

They are:

Lee 218	$\frac{1}{8}$ C.T. Blue
Lee 203	$\frac{1}{4}$ C.T. Blue
Lee 202	$\frac{1}{2}$ C.T. Blue
Lee 201	Full C.T. Blue

These colors are also useful to create natural daylight. Normal daylight is not yellow (as one may imagine a light source from the sun to be); neither is it white. Try to create daylight on a stage with white light, and, no matter how bright this artificial light, if a shaft of natural daylight were able to come through a window directly on to the stage, then, by comparison, the stage lighting would look very creamy in color.

Add one of the above gels (the choice depends on the level of light required), and a color far closer to natural daylight can be reproduced.

The choice of color for a designer is endless. Apart from the enormous range of colors to be found in the manufacturers' color books, all these different shades can, of course, be mixed. This can be done by putting two colors in one luminaire. For more interest, a composite color can be made.

Making a composite color

A composite color is created by cutting different pieces of gel (or color filter) to fit one color frame. This can be used to great effect with a gobo, perhaps, for instance, to simulate autumn leaves. It is important that the main crossover of color should be in the center of the color frame, as this is where the beams of light emitted from the lens are most concentrated. When they are finally arranged, the colors can be fixed together with cellophane tape.

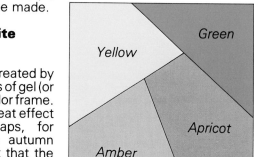
Incorrect composite

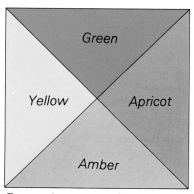
Four-color composite

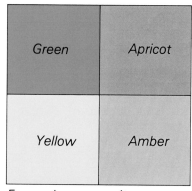
Four-color composite

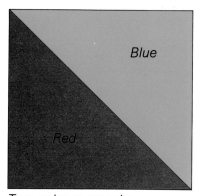
Two-color composite

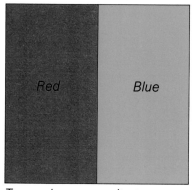
Two-color composite

Depending on the type of color used, sometimes one of the colors in the composition may shrink or wrinkle with the heat. When this happens, it usually destroys the whole frame of color. This may be avoided if a piece of clear gel (called a sacrificial gel) is placed behind the frame of composite color and in front of the lens. This gel will help to absorb some of the heat and thus reduce the wrinkling effect.

A lighting color wheel

This wheel shows some of the colors that might be used for stage lighting. These are all fairly intense colors and, if used for lighting an acting area, the hues would be far less saturated. (This means they would be closer to white.)

Warm and cool colors are shown on opposite halves of the wheel but there is the added complication that the yellowish-green and lavender shades could be defined under either category, depending upon the color against which they are contrasted.

Filters may be made of dyed gelatine, plastic, or polyester, or colored glass. Cinemoid is a cellulose acetate, which is very useful as it is self-extinguishing and therefore it does not constitute a fire risk.

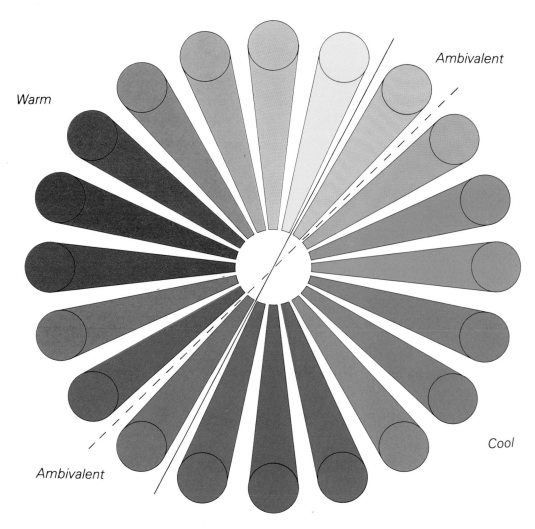

Warm

Ambivalent

Ambivalent

Cool

Choosing color

It is very difficult to give advice on what color to use for given circumstances. So much will depend on set and costume color, the director's ideas, conditions in the theater, and on the particular requirements of each show. However, here are a few basic guidelines which may be of help.

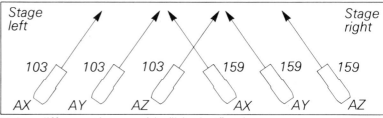
Using different tints avoids "blanket" color

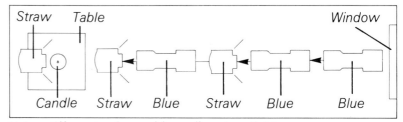
Using different colors adds realism to a light source

The use of tints has already been discussed . When dealing with these, it will add to the general molding quality of the light if a different tint is used on each side. For instance, if a straw-tint front light is definitely required, it will look less like a flat blanket color if Lee 103 (straw) is used on one side and Lee 159 (straw tint) on the other

This can, of course, be taken a stage further when a designer is working from obvious light sources. Imagine, for instance, a room with a candlelight source on stage right, and an open window with moonlight on stage left. Two totally different colors may be used in the side light, perhaps a straw from stage right to left, and a blue from stage left to right.

The use of color in this way should greatly enhance all the sculpturing qualities of the scene, and also gives a sense of direction to the illumination.

It is important that the lighting designer does not "mush" the visual appearance of a scene. This will happen if the overall wash of color combines too closely with the set, so that it all looks rather bland and boring, like a thick soup.

For example, if a set designer chooses a bamboo color for the set, the costume designer may then follow this theme through and select a range of beige-colored costumes. The lighting designer could well think that, in order to enhance all these straw-type colors, the scene should also be lit in straw. This would be heading down the road to disaster.

Such a combination would take on a "mushy" feel, with actors and set combining and thus becoming difficult to look at.

Instead, a crisp, sharp back-light color should be used to separate the actors from the set. A front light of, perhaps, just plain white, used with this combination of colors, could look surprisingly warm and would certainly help to define the actors.

Only experience, practice, and experimenting with different gels can make a lighting designer more confident when choosing color.

Perhaps the best advice is to "play safe" when first lighting plays. Generally, it is better to do the following:

Light with tints from the front, and leave any heavier colors for the back or side light.

When lighting with the same color from both sides, use different shades of that color to add interest.

Beware of using a blanket color wash which is the same tone as the set and costumes.

Color is a marvellous tool for the lighting designer — if it is used with care. Try to be aware of the effects of light and color all around you.

Simply because color can have a sensational or very dramatic impact, so is it also true that even quite small subtle changes in it can alter the atmosphere — both in the real world, and on the stage.

Color in action

Ring Round the Moon

The rig consisted of a two-color wash from the front, with 52 (pale gold) and 54 (pale rose) being used for pink skin toning, and Lee 201 (full CT) and 61 (slate blue) for blue toning. It also incorporated a blue backlight wash 63 (sky blue), as well as a very pale yellow (Lee 212 LCT).

The design called for the stage floor surrounding the set to be colored in deep blue for the night scenes, and also the actors needed to be illuminated by light emanating from a house off stage left. For this purpose, a boom of low cross light was placed behind each side flat on stage left. Chromoid 98 (bastard amber) was used in the cross light, which lit the actors seen stage left but not the floor. This was lit by the blue back light.

A white cyclorama was used and this was lit by Chromoid 93 in front of 1 kilowatt tungsten-halogen floodlights. On some occasions a string of Chinese lanterns had to appear to illuminate the stage. In order to reinforce this effect, the area inside the set was covered by a wash of break-up gobos with varying composite colors.

Kipling

The rig construction of *Kipling* was designed in such a way that the man, Kipling, (who was portrayed by Alec McCowen) could be highlighted effectively or followed wherever he moved on the stage.

This was achieved by normal area separation (described on pages 76–81) and each area

Ring Round the Moon

Kipling

was lit in the following manner: The front light consisted of Lee 203 ($\frac{1}{4}$ CT) and open white. A sepia toning was required and this was obtained by "toppy" side light (that is side light which is moving slightly towards overhead lighting), colored in Lee 205 ($\frac{1}{2}$ CT orange) and Lee 204 (full CT orange).

The rear projector seen in the photograph provided constantly changing effects, but also often reverted to the original slide's image of a window. For this purpose a backlight wash of Lee

202 ($\frac{1}{2}$ CT) was used to imitate daylight from behind.

The photograph actually shows the "preset", which had its own set of "specials"; a down or toplight wash of zenith blue (gelatran 60), and a "special" focused on each of the furniture pieces. The luminaires were set just down stage of the "180 degree relationship" to each piece, so as to strike the front of the articles. Lee 203 was used in each "special" to diminish the creaminess of the white light at low level.

Color in action

When the Wind Blows

Because of the restricted area separation plan, the coloring of each area varied a great deal. The living room had a two-color frontlight wash of Lee 162 (bastard amber) and Lee 201 (full GT). The kitchen had a front wash of 73 (half straw) and 45 (daylight blue). There was a sidelight wash of 54 (pale rose) in the living room to mimic light-bounce from the rosy walls; a side light of 3 (straw) in the kitchen (where the walls were yellow) served the same purpose in this area.

The outside area was lit, in the main, with Lee tungsten-to-daylight filters (201-3 and 218). This gave clarity at all levels with the 201 producing a good graying color at low level to add to the effect after the bomb had been dropped.

Peter Pan

The nursery scene pictured here was lit and colored in a fairly natural way to save the "magic" for later in the show. A warm and cool frontlight wash was used; pink (52 pale gold) and blues (45 daylight blue and 40 pale blue).

As most of the scenes were at night, a very "toppy" side light was used for highlighting each area in a composite color of 32 (medium blue) and 63 (sky blue). The side lighting consisted of a three-color wash, using amber, pink, and blue respectively. These were numbers 2 (light amber), 78 (salmon pink) and gelatran 60 (zenith blue). A backlight wash of gelatran 64 (medium blue) completed the main-rig construction.

When the Wind Blows

Peter Pan

The picture shows the use of a warm front light in pale gold, cooled just slightly by the blue front light to improve its clarity. The medium-blue back light produced blue halos when room lights were switched off, so as to imitate the moonlight through the windows. Extra pink toning from the side (to simulate the night lights above the bed), was provided by 2-kilowatt Fresnels colored in Lee 157 (pink) and set on each downstage perch. This pink highlighting can be seen in the white sheeting. The color structuring in this picture shows perhaps the least complicated coloring used in the show.

The Bengal Lancer

The set of *The Bengal Lancer*, which was designed by Bob Crowley, consisted of twenty-five tons of sand, a large amount of gauze, and a few set pieces. This simple but very effective approach to the set left a good deal of scope for the lighting designer.

The photograph here was taken in The Studio at the Haymarket Theatre in Leicester, where fairly limited lighting resources applied. Its subsequent transfer to The Lyric in London enabled the production to erect a rather more elaborate rig, while still retaining the same color format.

The sand, which was reddish in color, was lit by top light in Lee 238 This added extra "heat" to the appearance of the play, which, for the most part, was set in India. The gauzes were lit in blues and pale mauves and contrasted well with the rear cyclorama, which was lit in salmon colors (as shown in the photograph).

The transfer to the Lyric allowed the opportunity to reverse these colors and use salmon gauzes and a blue or mauve cyclorama, as well as the original colors. This provided for greater variation and heightened the effect of different localities within the show.

The set pieces were lit as individual sections in side, top, and front light, and the varying colors were used to create variety in the show because, although the set did not change, the localities, the time of day, and the seasons of the year, did alter considerably.

There was just one cover of front light in warm tints (not shown here). Lee 103 was used from one side, and Lee 162 from the other. Any cooling of colors was achieved by the pale-blue side light, which was colored in Lee 203 and Lee 202 ($\frac{1}{4}$ and $\frac{1}{2}$ CT).

The Bengal Lancer

Color in action

The Gondoliers

Opera can be one of the most exciting forms of theater for a lighting designer. It usually offers scope for a wide choice of color and light angles within lavish sets. This is one time when the lighting designer will probably need to pay as much attention to lighting the set as to the acting area.

The set shown here from *The Gondoliers (Act Two)*, has eleven flown pieces, each of which was separately lit. The colors used were two-fold, one selection to enhance the color of the set, and the other to exaggerate these chosen colors. For instance, to enhance the color of amber on the borders, Chromoid 98 (pale golden amber) was used, but to exaggerate it yet further, Chromoid 134 (golden amber) was also used. The coloring on the walls was designed using the same principle, graduating to the color of the floor.

1 The Gondoliers

There were several dance numbers in the show and when these were taking place, a full awareness of the set was unnecessary. The photo here shows the dancers isolated within the set, which is just visible behind. The color used here included a blue Chromoid 93 for back light, which gave a deep overall color to the stage. A low cross light of L117 (steel blue) from stage right and Cinemoid 69 (ariel blue) from stage left gave the dancers extra form. As the lights were focused straight across the stage and shuttered from the floor, the deep-blue back light, which illuminated the stage floor, was not affected. A wash

2 Dancers isolated within the set

110

of Lee 162 was used at low level from the front to enhance all the skin tones.

As can be seen in this photograph, the set for Act One presented a lighting problem; side light could not be used from off stage, except from a downstage perch position.

The scene here, showing the actors "in song", was left in a fairly "normal" lighting state. Because of the pastel-colored costumes, great care had to be taken not to destroy their delicate shades by using lighting which was too heavy.

Light tints were used to front light in warm and cool, using Lee 162 and Cinemoid 45 (daylight blue). Side light from the perches was in a very light blue to add further clarity (as can be seen in the highlighting of the actors downstage left). The border of painted washing was lit with Lee 218 ($\frac{1}{2}$ C.T.) which simply color-corrected the white light, allowing the natural color of the painted washing to show through. The floor coloring was created by the back light, thus ensuring that the actors' faces and costume fronts were not affected. Although the back light was fairly heavy and used deep blues (Chromoid 93), primary reds (Chromoid 106), and deep orange (Chromoid 158), a fairly neutral back light was achieved by mixing them.

3 Actors in song

Special effects

Put quite simply, special effects are fun! Whatever aspect of production may be concerned, whether set design, properties, makeup, or the lighting, any departure from the routine or humdrum is always welcome; as such, special effects can be particularly exciting and very rewarding for all involved. They provide a good opportunity to be inventive and to use one's imagination to the full!

There are, of course, bound to be a few problems and frustrations, as with any other area of lighting, but perhaps the greatest difficulty of all is knowing when to stop! It is always a temptation to overdo a special effect, particularly if it has been rather difficult or expensive to contrive. There may be a grim determination to use it to the full, to the detriment of the overall end result.

None the less, when producing and using special effects, the lighting designer has a unique opportunity to be creative and ingenious. Do experiment with different methods, both old and new, and explore all the various techniques and pieces of equipment that are available to you. If conventional methods will not produce exactly what is required, then a new special effect may have to be invented. The scope is enormous.

Many special effects are described in this chapter. These include the moon and stars, rain, lightning, and swirling clouds; rippling water, fire-effects and neon signs. Some are produced by technical means, such as projection, gobos, and ripple machines. Others need only very simple equipment, such as light boxes or a gauze screen, while a stunning galaxy of stars requires only foil and black cotton thread.

Not all the special effects discussed in this chapter are strictly "lighting". They have nevertheless been included, because it is usually the lighting department, with all its technical know-how, that is asked to stretch its limits and produce the very wide variety of effects that may be needed.

Stars

Making stars

Stars can be created in number of ways, and which method is best to use really depends on the design and restrictions of the set concerned.

Projecting stars

Stars can be projected. This can be done by using a star slide in a projector, or by fitting a star gobo into a profile luminaire.

Using a star cloth

Stars can be "wired" into a cloth. The stars are, in fact, made up of pea bulbs, or any pin-point light source. A small hole is pierced in the cloth and the bulb is then poked through. It can be successfully wired from the back. This method is obviously very time-consuming, but has the advantage of being both very effective and easily controllable. If the wiring of so many bulbs is too daunting a prospect, use instead a ready-made string of clear or white Christmas-tree bulbs.

Hanging stars

Hanging stars are made of balls of foil, attached to black cotton thread, and flown to the required height.

To create a "galaxy", simply tie a number of lengths of black cotton thread to the house bar at irregular intervals.

Now tear off pieces of foil and roll them up into $\frac{1}{4}$ inch (6mm) balls. They can then be attached to the lengths of black cotton thread by twisting them around the threads, being careful to avoid too regular a pattern.

When this is complete, the cotton thread can then be swagged to form a "galaxy".

By side, top, or up lighting the arrangement, the foil will be illuminated so as to twinkle effectively. The black cotton thread will be scarcely visible.

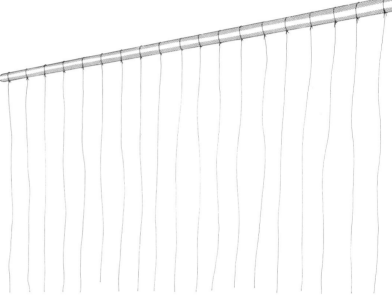

Black cotton thread hanging from house bar

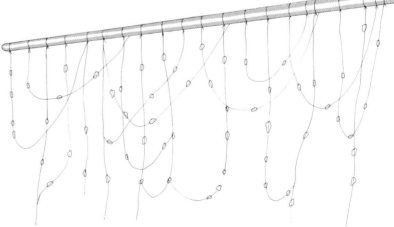

Using cotton thread with foil to make a galaxy

114

The moon

Projecting a moon

The most common method of creating a moon is to project it. If a full moon is required, a profile should be "irised" to give the correct size and then focused on the cyclorama or cloth. An acceptable full moon may be produced this way; a crescent moon can be created by using a gobo in the luminaire. It is important to remember when projecting a moon, that the light source should really be at right angles to the material on to which it will be projected. Otherwise a full moon ends up looking rather egg-shaped! This right angle is sometimes difficult to contrive from the front. Back projection may alleviate this problem, as the light unit remains unseen and can therefore be lowered to a suitable position without being compromised by having to hide behind part of the set.

Obviously if the cyclorama or cloth is inclined at an angle (as in *The Recruiting Officer,* discussed on pages 166-71), then the position of light must follow suit in order to maintain the correct angle.

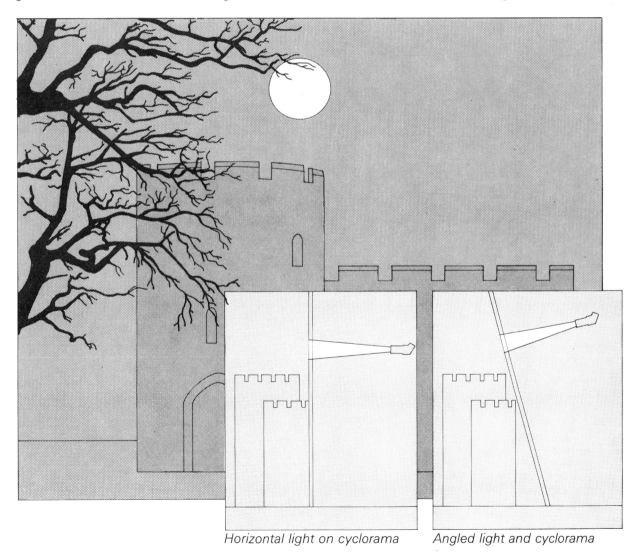

Horizontal light on cyclorama   *Angled light and cyclorama*

Using a light box

Another method of creating a moon is by using a "light box".

This is simply what its name suggests — a source of light contained within a box. It is usually made of wood with the front removed, and fitted with lamps, which are wired into the box unit.

The type of lamp used will largely depend on the depth of the box and the brightness required. If a shallow box is used, strip-lights will be the best option as then the whole light fitting will be suitably narrow. If a deeper box is chosen, domestic light bulbs can be inserted. Pearlized bulbs will help diffuse the light. Even so, there may be some hot spots. This can be alleviated if silver-top (or reflector-top) bulbs are used instead.

The front of the light box can be covered to suit the design requirements. Often the front is made of calico which will help to disperse the light over the whole area. If the light box is being used to create a moon, then a piece of black card or wood can be cut to the required shape, depending on how full the moon is meant to be. This is then fitted to the front of the light box.

A light box of this type (now made into a moon box) is usually hung directly behind a cyclorama or backcloth. It is important that the box is positioned so that it is virtually touching the cloth or it will not create a sharp enough image.

This is probably the best method of creating a moon, as any shape can be quite easily produced, and there are no distortion problems. Of course, the light box can be used for many other different effects. Any shape can be cut, or fretted, out of a wooden sheet and then fitted to the front of a light box.

Neon signs

Light boxes are often used to make an effective illuminated sign when the set requires one. Color gels can be fitted between the box and its front cover to color the sign and to mimic the effect of neon. A frosted gel will help disperse hot spots.

Colored light bulbs can also be used to color the image on the front of the box. If there are two or three separate circuits of bulbs in the box, and each circuit is fitted with different colored bulbs,(perhaps red, yellow, and blue), these can be made to flash in order, so that the sign continually changes color.

A sun box

If the lighting box is to be used as a sun box (as opposed to a moon box), then the colors could be made to fade from whitish yellow to golden amber as the sun sets. The effect can be greatly enhanced by supporting the sun box on a flying line and then slowly lowering it down the back of the cyclorama, so the sun "sets".

If the particular color of bulb required cannot be readily purchased, then it is possible to paint an ordinary pearled bulb,or to dip it in FEV (French enamel varnish). Many different colors and tints are available.

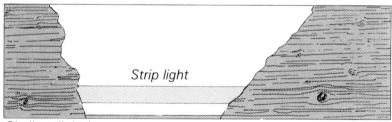

Strip light

Shallow light box

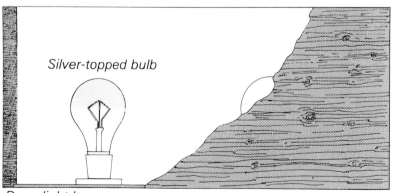

Silver-topped bulb

Deep light box

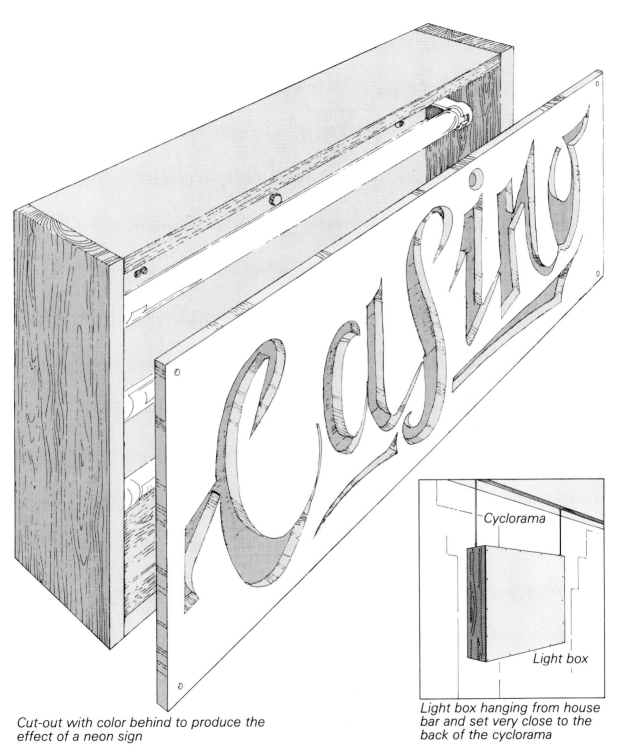

Cut-out with color behind to produce the effect of a neon sign

Light box hanging from house bar and set very close to the back of the cyclorama

Cyclorama

Light box

Clouds

If possible, try to utilize two different projectors, both fitted with a cloud effect, and then focus them on to the same area. Make sure that one effect is running at a slightly faster speed than the other. The clouds will then move across each other and this will result in a more realistic effect.

If the projection is to be directed on to a cyclorama or a sky-cloth, then it is a good idea to obtain a gauze (scrim) and then set this just down stage of the cloth. By projecting on to the gauze, an image will be created on both the gauze and the cyclorama, as the light passes through the mesh of the gauze. This creates a wonderful 3-D effect.

Clouds across a moon

Unfortunately, if a moon effect has been used (as described earlier on pages 115-6), then simply projecting clouds across this will not give a true representation of how clouds move past the moon. This is because when clouds cross the moon they become silhouettes.

The only way to achieve this effect is by using two projectors with cloud effects. The first projector has a "positive mask" to project the moon and the clouds that go across it. The second projector will have a "negative mask" to project the clouds surrounding the moon.

The masks can be made from card or lithoplate. It will soon be discovered that the negative shape may be difficult to suspend in the center of the effect aperture. It may therefore be best to paint the masking required on to clear acetate which can be far more easily taped into position.

Even when using an identical cloud disc for each effect, the cloud images will be unlikely to completely coincide. It is impossible to fully co-ordinate the way they enter, cross, and leave the moon. This really does not matter, however, for it would take a very keen eye to spot exactly what is happening.

The effect may be further enhanced if the projector producing the moon is set at a higher intensity than its negative counterpart. The lining up of the two projectors is critical; the positive and negative moons must overlay each other exactly.

Static clouds

Meshed gobos can be used to form very good clouds, if no movement is required. This is, in fact, the cheapest method of creating projected clouds because quite ordinary profile luminaires can be used, and there will be no need to hire a special projector.

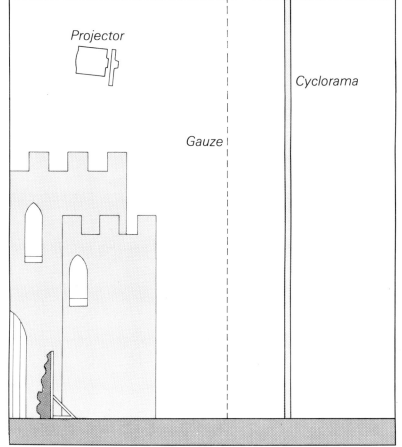

Using a gauze (scrim) and cyclorama creates a 3-D effect

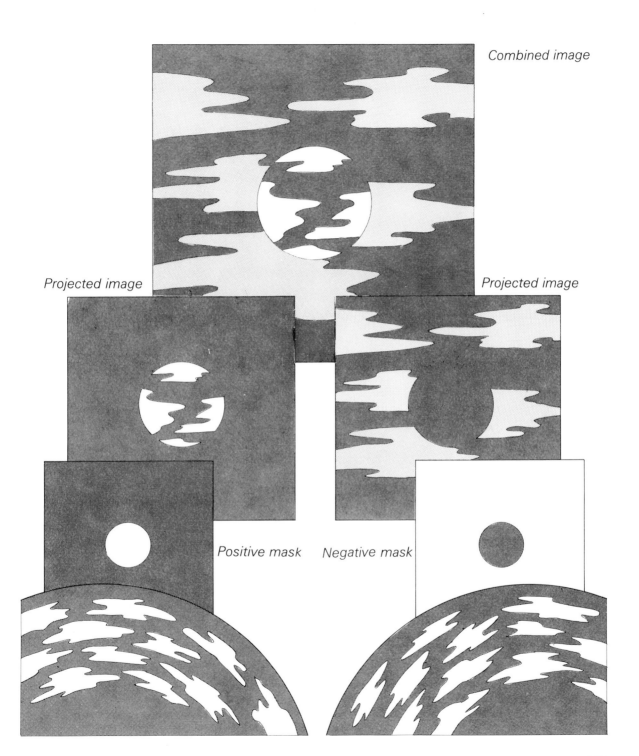

Combined image

Projected image

Projected image

Positive mask

Negative mask

Snow, water, and lightning

Snow

The most realistic snow effect is achieved by using a snow bag. The bag is set in the flies and from this overhead position, it releases hundreds of paper dots which float gently to the stage floor.

This method, however, is not always acceptable, because of the inevitable mess it causes! An alternative is to use a projected-snow effect, but this, unfortunately, often ends up looking rather ridiculous, largely because of its repetitive nature.

To some extent, this problem can be overcome by using two projectors focused on to the same area. If possible, try to obtain two snow-effect discs and make sure their dot formats are different.

A snow effect is achieved by using a glass disc which has been painted black, except for a pattern of clear dots. Light can pass through these little spaces and the pattern formed will look remarkably like snowflakes.

If the snow effects in the two projectors are run at different speeds, the illusion of falling snow will be rather more convincing. In this respect the effect is similar to a moving-cloud projection.

Water

There are several water effects available. These include running water, rain, waves, and ripples. The first two are usually created by using discs in the same way as for clouds or snow, but waves and ripples are effected rather differently.

A moving-water effect is created by fluted glass pieces. Instead of rotating as discs do, these glass pieces move up and down within the effects unit. The result is rather like gentle waves furrowing the surface of the sea.

Ripples can be made by using a ripple machine (or projector). This ripple machine consists of a rotating metal tube into which ripple patterns have been cut. A light source is fixed behind it and the two units are mounted in a metal case.

Forked lightning

If forked lightning has to be projected on to a cyclorama or over a set, then the most convenient method is to use a forked-lightning gobo set which is inserted into a profile spotlight. Some manufacturers (or rental companies) may convert a profile luminaire to incorporate a strobe bulb. This, in turn, must be plugged into a strobe unit. The high-intensity flash given by the strobe bulb greatly enhances the forked-lightning effect.

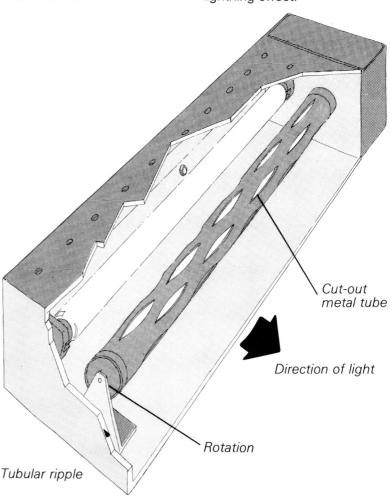

Cut-out metal tube

Direction of light

Rotation

Tubular ripple

Strobes, light curtains, and gauze transformations

Strobes

Stroboscopic lights work on a "captive-discharge" principle. Strobes can be used very successfully to simulate any flashing-light effect, and they are particularly dramatic when imitating film on an antiquated projector or when used to make actors appear to be performing in an old-fashioned silent movie.

A word of warning, however, is needed here. Strobes must be used only with extreme caution and only for very short periods of time. There are, in fact, legal requirements regarding this and these should be checked. Apart from the unpleasant effect on the eyes and the sense of balance, they may induce an epileptic fit. Some insertion in the program to give prior warning of their use is essential — and then keep well within the maximum time allowed.

Light curtains

A light curtain is, as the name suggests, simply a curtain of light. Lighting designers in the "pop-music" industry have used light curtains for many years. They have a very powerful and dramatic effect, especially when a number are used, one behind another in lots of different colors.

Light curtains may be usefully employed in theater lighting. (A description of how a light curtain was used in *When the Wind Blows* is included on pages 175-6.) A light curtain is produced by a row of Par lamps directly next to each other. They can be separate Par cans (see page 32) or combined units which make a batten of Par

Elevation of a light curtain

lights. These battens of Pars may be of the low-voltage type. Whichever sort they are, the object is that each unit must give an intense, near-parallel beam of light.

The batten or row of Pars is set at an angle, pointing towards the audience (so this is, in effect, back lighting). The steeper the angle, the better the result will be.

The intense light the Pars provide will illuminate any dust or dirt particles floating in the atmosphere, as they are "caught" in the beam. The more dense the dust or dirt, the better the effect. Wafting smoke through the atmosphere will make it "dirtier" and it will then be virtually impossible to see through the light beams. Thus, apart from the visual impact a light curtain creates, it can also be put to a practical use. It will effectively mask whatever lies up stage of it, so a scene change can therefore be hidden behind a light curtain, or an actor might "appear from nowhere" through the veil of light.

Gauze transformations

Used skilfully, a gauze (or scrim) transformation can really create magical effects. Through what appears at first to be a solid scenic cloth, a whole scene can materialize quite unexpectedly. However, the lighting of a scenic gauze must be done very carefully to achieve the "magic" successfully.

Whether or not the gauze is painted, the steeper the angle of light which illuminates it, the better the result. If the gauze does not incorporate a painted design, then back lighting can be considered. The main objective is to prevent too much light passing through the mesh of the gauze and illuminating whatever is up stage of it. Lighting the gauze in this way will make it appear solid.

Any actors, magical scenes, or new sets that are to be lit and seen through the gauze must, of course, always be lit by luminaires that have been set up stage of the gauze. It is essential to remember this when planning the rig.

Very careful timing will be needed as the lights are brought up on the scene behind and simultaneously reduced on the gauze in front so that the change-over can take place perfectly smoothly. The stage will then appear to be suddenly and mysteriously transformed, as if a solid medium has melted away and a new scene has been conjured from nowhere.

The effect is really so simple to perform and yet it can lend quite a stunning or beautiful element to a scene.

Gobos (patterns)

Gobos (or cookies) are not used solely for special effects, but are often an integral part of the main rig. Sometimes they may be used so subtly that the audience are quite unaware of their presence. On the other hand, their impact may be so striking that they become an effect in themselves.

As explained earlier (on page 29), a gobo is a metal plate with whatever shape is required cut or etched out of it. The size of the plate will depend upon the luminaire for which the gobo is intended. The determining factor is the gate size of the luminaire, as this is where the gobo (or an iris or mask) will be fitted. The shape that has been cut in the metal plate can then be successfully fitted and projected in a profile luminaire. Some other types of luminaire are unsuitable as the gobo must be inserted between the light source and the focusing lens.

Projecting images and texturing

Gobos are most commonly used to project the images of windows, tree branches, or leaves; or to create "break-up" patterns on the stage.

Break-up refers to a method of texturing which can be very useful when lighting a set or stage floor. A piece of scenery, or perhaps a wall or house front, may look rather bland if it is simply washed with plain light. This is particularly so if the surface is flat. Lighting the surface with break-up gobos and using an appropriate soft focus will add texture and interest. This can be further

enhanced by the use of a composite color (see page 104). A simple break-up gobo will consist of just a metal plate which has been drilled with a series of random holes. Leaf gobos, intended primarily to create woodland effects, can also be used for very simple texturing, provided that the luminaire is suitably defocused.

Almost any shape can be projected with a gobo. Many shapes are readily available from gobo manufacturers and come complete with their respective holders. Three examples are shown below.

If the required shape is not available, manufacturers will usually etch them to order.

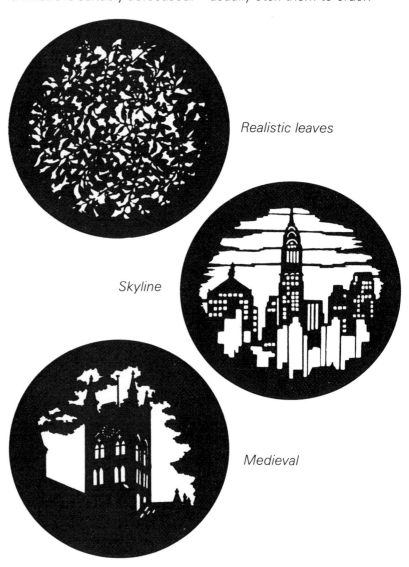

Realistic leaves

Skyline

Medieval

Making a gobo

Gobos can be quite expensive, so it may be worthwhile attempting to make a simple gobo yourself. All that is required is some thin metal, preferably aluminum-based, so that it will be easy to cut. Printers' lithoplate is ideal. If this is not available, then the base of foil plates or trays (perhaps from the local "take-away" restaurant) will suffice.

First cut from the lithoplate or foil tray a piece of metal that will suit the gate size of the luminaire — it is advisable to make the piece a few inches taller than the gate size so it can be easily fitted and removed.

Next cut out the particular shape required. If it is to be used as a break-up gobo, then simply drill or punch holes all over the plate. If, on the other hand, a specific shape is needed, then this should be cut out with a very sharp knife or a Stanley blade. Begin at the center of the metal piece and be careful not to cut too near the edges or some of the shape may be lost during the focusing.

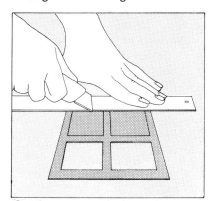

Cutting out a window shape with a modeling knife

Composite gobos

Gobos can be used to create a composite effect to make, for example, a projected stained-glass window. These can be achieved most effectively by using a special composite gobo set, made specifically for this purpose. This set usually consists of four or five gobos, each of which will create one piece of stained-glass window.

Each of these gobos must be fitted to a separate luminaire, but every one of these luminaires must be of exactly the same type. The images projected from these luminaires are then focused one on top of another, until a complete stained-glass window effect is formed. By putting a different color filter into each luminaire, a very realistic and attractive effect can be achieved.

Green

Yellow

Blue

Red

White

Complete window

Gobos

Creating moving images with gobos

Surprisingly, gobos can also be used to make a moving image. The method is similar to that used for composite effects. To create, for example, a water fountain, four gobos would be used. The first of these will be cut into a fountain shape, and the other three will have been pierced with water droplet shapes. The droplets should be cut out in slightly different places on each of these three gobos, so that their respective positions fall progressively lower on each gobo.

Once again four luminaires are required, and each will be fitted with one of the gobos. Focus each projected image so that it overlays the others. Every luminaire must have its own circuit. Then the lights can be made to chase each other. By quickly flashing each luminaire in turn, the water appears to move. The light in the luminaire which contains the basic fountain structure, will, of course, remain constant.

Using mesh in gobos

The use of fine mesh in the manufacture of gobos is now becoming very popular. This mesh will allow shapes to be suspended in the middle of another design, and very realistic clouds can also be made by using this method.

A word of warning is again necessary here. Gobos are fitted to one of the hottest parts of a profile spotlight. The center of a gobo will very quickly heat up and glow red hot. Extreme care must be taken when fitting or removing them. If the luminaire involved has been on, even if for only a very short time, always use gloves or a cloth to handle the gobo or its holder.

A mesh-tone cloud gobo

Projection

There are a number of very good special effects that can be projected. These are readily available and can be very useful. (Scenic projection has not been included in this discussion but the notes regarding angle distortion at the end of this section will apply to most forms of projection.)

A lighting designer may be called upon to create "moving" effects as well as static ones. Often some movement will be needed to add to the natural appearance of clouds, snow, water, smoke, and fire.

In most cases, a call to a local theater rental firm will secure a suitable projector and effects unit. In principle, the mechanics are the same for all the various types of projector and effect. All you will need to know is the wattage of light required from the projector, the throw (the distance from projection to image), and the image size. It is from the throw and image data that the objective lens size is calculated. Provided the type of projector and the "gate" size is known, it will be possible to work out the lens size.

As a guide, if the projector is using a 3 inch x 3 inch (75mm x 75mm) gate, then the lens size can be calculated by using the chart on the right.

Thus, there are three units which make up the total effect. These are the projector (or light source), the effect, and the objective lens.

The effect must be fitted to the front of the projector, and the lens must then be fitted to the front of the effect.

Most moving effects are simply produced by using a painted glass disc which rotates by means of a motor inside the effects unit. The painting will represent the image which is to be projected, such as clouds, running water, fire, smoke, or falling snow.

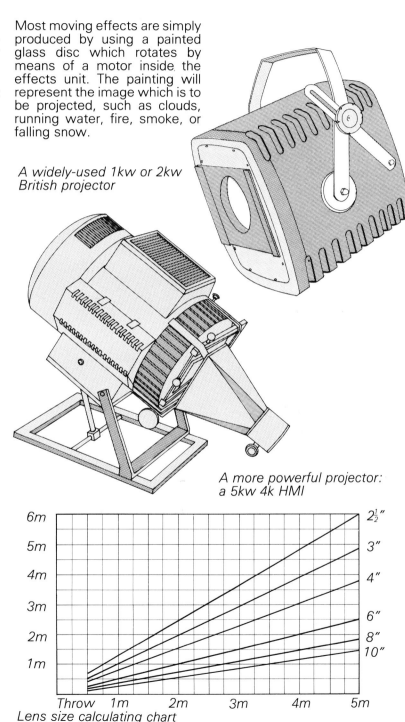

A widely-used 1kw or 2kw British projector

A more powerful projector: a 5kw 4k HMI

Lens size calculating chart

125

◇ Pyrotechnics

It must be pointed out that maroons, flash powder, and transformation powder are all potentially dangerous and if used or stored incorrectly, then an explosion or fire could result. Always be sure to follow these instructions in order to maintain safety standards.

1 In the UK, a licence is required before explosives can be kept or stored. Check with your local fire or police department and follow any advice given.

2 It is advisable to contact the fire or police department, in any event, to see whether you can actually use pyrotechnics (The building where the production is to take place may be deemed unsuitable for such a potentially dangerous exercise.)

3 Always store the pyrotechnics in a metal container when they are not in use, and preferably in a room that has been set aside and labeled "Explosives Store"; so that no-one can be in any doubt as to the nature of the contents therein.

4 **Never** smoke when using, wiring, or loading flash boxes; or when handling transformation powder or flash powder.

5 **Always** unplug the flash box or device you are working on.

6 Mark clearly all plugs and switches that will be operating any explosive device and then make sure everyone concerned is warned about them.

7 Follow the manufacturers' instructions to the full.

Maroons

Maroons are used to create the noise of explosions by actually exploding. They come in three basic sizes which contain varying amounts of an explosive material encased in cardboard. They are somewhat similar in construction to a "banger" type firework. They are electrically detonated by using a special pyrotechnics detonator, and easily fired from an ordinary small six-volt battery.

Bomb tank

Maroons must always be placed in a suitable, metal open-ended container such as a dustbin or galvanized water tank, to contain the explosion. The open part of the "bomb tank" can be covered with chicken wire to prevent any large pieces of maroon leaving the tank, but never put the maroon into a completely closed container or it may well be turned into a potentially dangerous bomb!

If more than one explosion is required during a show, then more than one maroon can be placed in the bomb tank, and wired back to a separate switch. Sometimes, however, one maroon may destroy another when detonated. This can be prevented by placing the maroons as far apart from each other as possible.

Do make sure that everyone involved in the production, whose activities might take them in the vicinity of the bomb tank, knows exactly where it is and when the maroons are going to be detonated; then, hopefully, the area can be kept clear at the appropriate time.

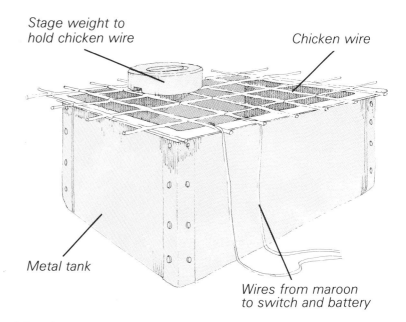

Stage weight to hold chicken wire

Chicken wire

Metal tank

Wires from maroon to switch and battery

A bomb tank

Flash powder

Flash powder is a very fast-burning powder which is used to create flashes. It is highly inflammable and great care must be taken when it is handled, so it is important to keep it well away from any open flame or strong heat sources.

Flash box

A flash box is used to contain the flash powder prior to and during the detonation and is made of metal. As the flash powder is usually ignited by remote control (usually from somewhere off-stage) the flash box contains two electrical terminals (live and neutral).

In the old days, the system was fairly primitive. The terminals would have been shorted out with a small piece of fuse wire, and a level teaspoon of flash powder was piled over the fuse wire. When the flash was required, the flash box was plugged into a mains supply, the fuse wire melted, and the flash powder was ignited. It was rather a case of keeping fingers crossed that the right wire melted and the building survived the experiment!

Nowadays one can hire or buy a flash-box system that is rather more sophisticated and reliable. It uses a premade flash cartridge that simply plugs into the flash box. It is detonated from a low-voltage power supply, situated in the switch box containing the "fire" button.

Pyrotechnic fuse or detonators

Pyrotechnic fuses can be used to detonate flash powder but their explosive force is very directional so the flash powder must be placed in just the right position. However, by using cigarette papers, it is quite a simple matter to make a home-made flash cartridge.

First, roll the cigarette paper around a pencil and then stick the glued edges together as normal. Put the pyro-fuse in one end of the paper cylinder, with the wires outermost, and then twist the paper around the wires to hold the paper on to the detonator. Pour flash powder in at the other end of the cylinder until it is almost full. Finish making the cartridge by twisting the paper together to hold the flash powder safely inside. The home-made cartridge can then be placed in a metal box and wired to a switch and battery.

Premade cartridge systems and pyro-fuses can turn out to be very expensive if a great many flashes are required. It may be considerably cheaper to use resistors as detonators and a car battery as a power supply. If $\frac{1}{4}$ watt 10 ohm carbon resistors are used, then the car battery should have no trouble in "blowing" the resistor.

Transformation powder

Transformation powder is a slow-burning powder which can produce a colored flame. Several colors are available and some, such as green and amber, can be very effective.

Transformation powder must not be mixed with the fast-burning flash powder because the force of the latter may send out a shower of the powder when it is still burning. It should therefore be held in a metal container and lit by a taper.

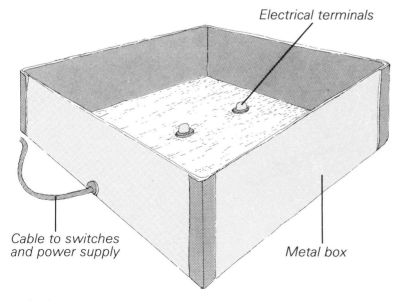

Electrical terminals

Cable to switches and power supply

Metal box

A flash box

Dry ice and smoke

Dry ice

Dry ice is frozen carbon dioxide. Gloves must be worn when handling dry ice as it sticks to the skin and burns. Also, when breaking up blocks, cover the ice with a sack or cloth to prevent splinters flying about and injuring someone's eyes.

When dry ice is melted in boiling water, the resulting vapor is heavier than air and will therefore hang near the ground. Special containers called dry-ice machines are available for sale or hire. These incorporate an electric element to boil water and consist, in effect, of a sealed box with one small opening from which the vapour escapes. A "cage" is included to hold the dry ice and, to some extent, the effect can be regulated by lowering or raising the cage in and out of the boiling water. These machines are designed to provide large amounts of vapor, but they can be expensive to buy. A small bath tub which is filled about half full of hot water and set on a trolley will provide the same effect. Never overfill the tub as the action of dry ice melting is extremely violent.

To assist the production of vapor, it is a good idea to break up the dry ice into small pieces. The greater the surface area available to the hot water, the better the reaction. Wrap the dry ice in a cloth or sack to avoid any pieces flying around, and then hit it with a hammer.

Storage

Storing dry ice can cause problems. If you put it in a domestic freezer, any food will be ruined and the dry ice will still deteriorate. The best method of storage is to seal the dry ice in an airtight plastic bag and then embed this in a box full of expanded polystyrene. This may keep the dry ice stable for a day or two. Really, the only way to ensure that there is always enough dry ice available for a performance is to collect it from the supplier a few hours before each night's show.

Smoke

Smoke can be created in a number of ways. The safest method is to use a smoke gun. Glycerine oil is forced through a heated pipe by either a CO_2 gas bottle or by an integral air-pressure pump. This smoke gun will produce vaporized glycerine oil which looks and acts very much like smoke. However, it does smell rather sweet and, unfortunately, it will also cover everything in a fine layer of glycerine oil.

Another smoke gun which is available can be easily refilled by simply screwing on a "spare can". These refills can be selected from a small range of different types of smoke effect. Each effect will look different according to how long the smoke stays in the air before finally dispersing. For example, one type will produce a "steaming kettle" effect, when the smoke disperses almost instantly; while another provides a lingering effect, to suggest, say, a misty morning. Thus, smoke guns are ideal for many effects, either to provide copious amounts of smoke, to swirl gently over the stage; or perhaps to "seed" the air so light beams are seen more clearly.

Smaller amounts of smoke can be made by heating a "slow burning" smoke powder on a heating element. This is not a safe method and, moreover, the fumes produced may be rather strong smelling!

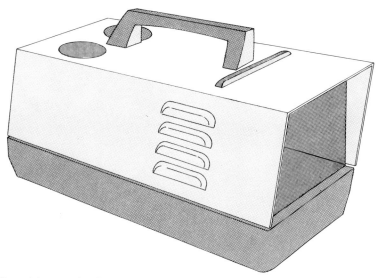

Portable smoke box

Flickering fires

An effective fire can be created by making a wooden grate and then using flickering colored light bulbs set behind it to give the impression of a glowing fire. By using fluorescent starters (which can be bought as spares for fluorescent light fittings) and wiring them in series with light bulbs, the bulbs can be made to flicker on and off indefinitely. The speed at which the bulb flickers can be altered by changing either the wattage size of the bulb or the starter. Use three or four different colored bulbs (to include red, yellow, and amber), with one on constantly and the others made to flicker; in this way an excellent copy of a real glowing fire will be created.

Fluorescent starters have only two connections and it does not matter which one is connected to the supply or bulb.

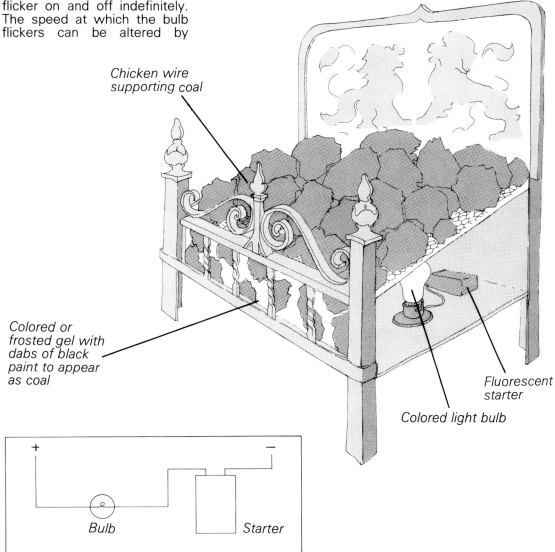

Chicken wire
supporting coal

Colored or
frosted gel with
dabs of black
paint to appear
as coal

Fluorescent
starter

Colored light bulb

Circuit diagram for wiring starter to light bulb

+   −

Bulb   Starter

Oil lamps

Electrically operated oil lamps

When a practical oil lamp is required on stage, the obvious way to control it is to use a mains-powered bulb fed via a dimmer, allowing the level of light output and the fading up or down to be controlled with the rest of the lighting rig. If, however, the oil lamp has to be carried around the stage by an actor during the show, it will then have to be battery operated. It is possible for the actor to fade the lamp up or down via a small potentiometer inserted in the oil lamp battery circuit. However, if the lamp has to work independently, then radio control is the answer.

Mains operated oil lamp

Use a pair of wire cutters to remove the wick and the mechanism for lowering and raising it, and then enough room can be made to fit a mains operated lamp holder. A gallery containing a lamp holder can also be bought to replace the wick gallery.

Battery operated oil lamp

Removing the wick and mechanism (as for the mains operated lamp) provides ample room for a small lamp holder such as an MES (Miniature Edison Screw). This can be securely fixed with either nuts and bolts or by binding it in with stiff wire. If this is done carefully, the space created by the removal of the controls to lower and raise the wick, should be sufficient to allow a potentiometer to be inserted. A wirewound potentiometer will be required for this.

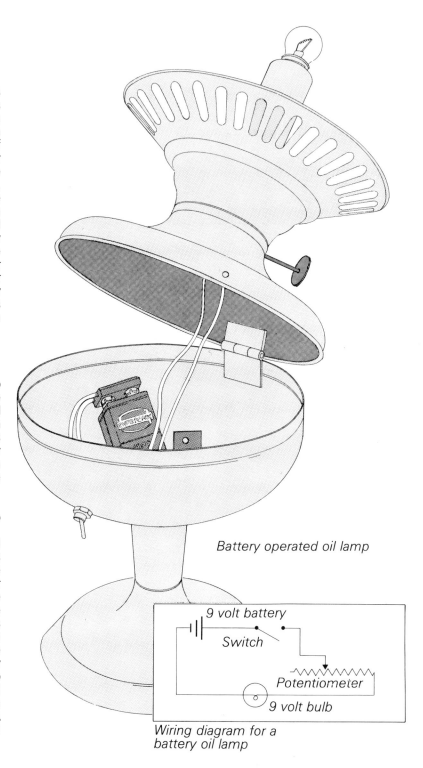

Battery operated oil lamp

Wiring diagram for a battery oil lamp

The only problem left is where to hide the batteries. The most obvious place is in the container that carries the oil, just below the gallery. It is quite likely that the opening that is left when the gallery is unscrewed is too small for the batteries to fit in, so the oil lamp will have to be modified to accept them. Using a hacksaw, cut very carefully around the container, just below the lip. Take care not to bend or scratch the lamp.

Now use a small brass hinge and carefully solder it to both pieces of the lamp, so that both parts will hinge open and close. Nuts and bolts with spacers could be used instead. These will prevent the lamp from, being bent out of shape when the flat hinge is fixed to the round lamp. At the opposite side of the lamp, fix a small piece of metal to the lid and drill a hole through this and through the bottom part of the lamp to make a catch to hold the two hinged parts together. The oil lamp can be opened to enable the batteries to be placed in the newly created, large opening compartment. A switch should then be inserted in the circuit to isolate the bulb from the battery and conserve energy.

Radio controlled oil lamp

Radio control equipment (as used in model kits) can be made to fade an oil lamp up and down. A transmitter, receiver, and DC motor speed controller are all that are needed. The DC motor-speed controller doubles as an excellent dimmer. Both receiver and speed controller can be hidden along with the batteries in the oil container. The aerial however should be kept outside

to avoid any loss of signal. It can be hidden, for instance, in the glass shade or funnel. The system can be used to run the standard torch bulb, as for the battery operated oil lamp. All the manufacturers' instructions should be followed in order to connect up the radio control equipment correctly. Make sure there is no interference.

Candles

Candles can be made very simply by using half (or one and a half) inch diameter, white plastic tubing, as found in a domestic water system. Simply fix a bulb in at one end with the wires feeding it running down the inside of the tube to a battery. If a candle tray is being used, this will effectively hide the switch and battery. A strip of tracing paper placed around the bulb and twisted into a flame shape, will make this candle look more realistic.

There are several electrical candles made for the theatre. One type can be bought in battery or mains form. It uses a specially shaped bulb which looks like a candle flame and is held in the candle on a tiny gimbel-like arrangement. This allows the bulb to move gently about as if the "flame" is wavering in the wind.

The other type uses the same PVC tubing as the home-made candle but it has an electronic circuit embedded in it. This produces a flicker between two bulbs built into the "flame" part of the candle. The effect created may appear a little wild, but it does resemble a candle in a strong wind. This candle can be run only from a 9v battery.

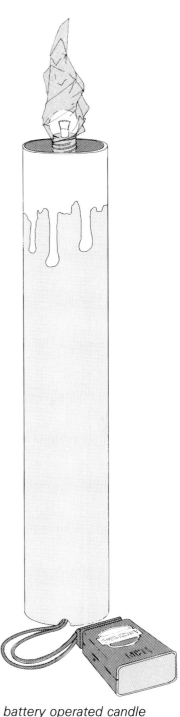

A battery operated candle

Notes on projection

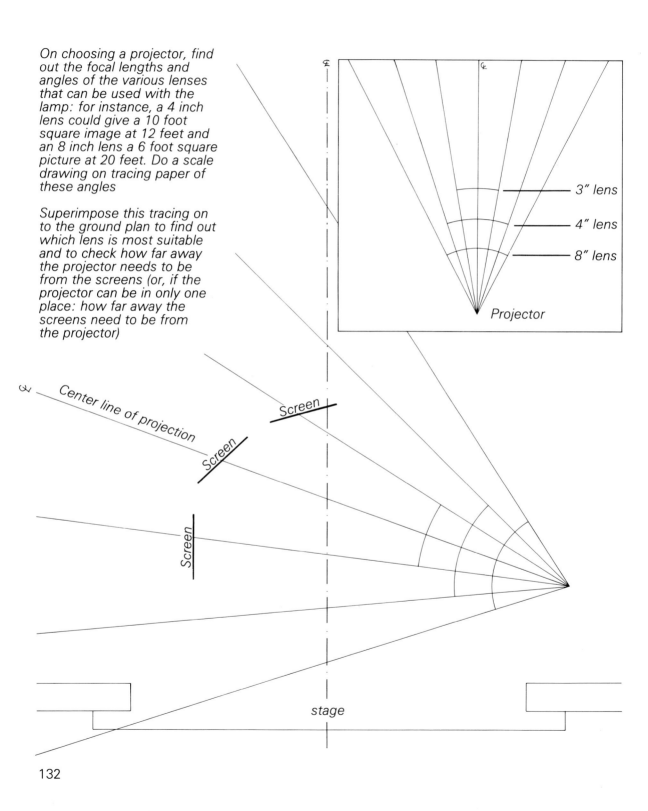

On choosing a projector, find out the focal lengths and angles of the various lenses that can be used with the lamp: for instance, a 4 inch lens could give a 10 foot square image at 12 feet and an 8 inch lens a 6 foot square picture at 20 feet. Do a scale drawing on tracing paper of these angles

Superimpose this tracing on to the ground plan to find out which lens is most suitable and to check how far away the projector needs to be from the screens (or, if the projector can be in only one place: how far away the screens need to be from the projector)

3" lens

4" lens

8" lens

Projector

Center line of projection

Screen

Screen

Screen

stage

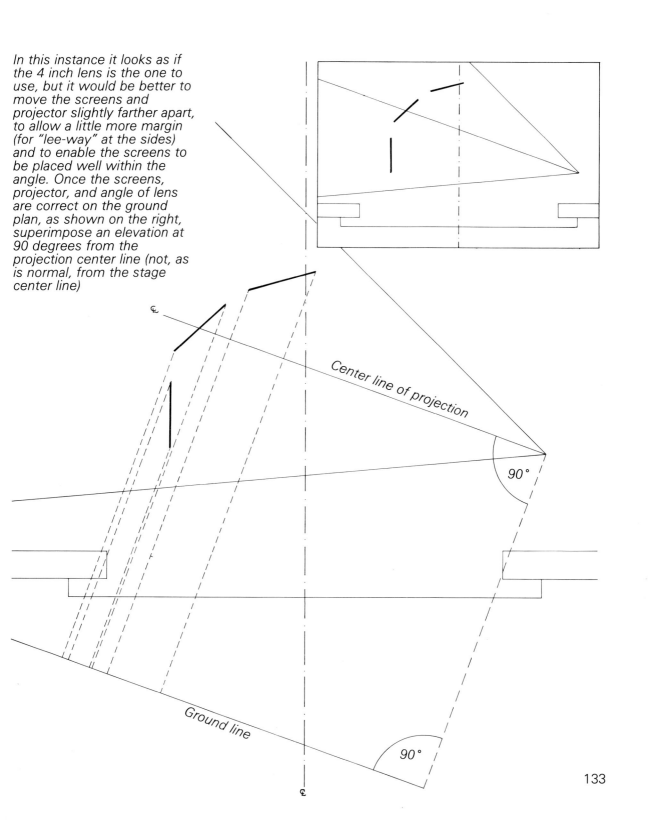

In this instance it looks as if the 4 inch lens is the one to use, but it would be better to move the screens and projector slightly farther apart, to allow a little more margin (for "lee-way" at the sides) and to enable the screens to be placed well within the angle. Once the screens, projector, and angle of lens are correct on the ground plan, as shown on the right, superimpose an elevation at 90 degrees from the projection center line (not, as is normal, from the stage center line)

Center line of projection

90°

Ground line

90°

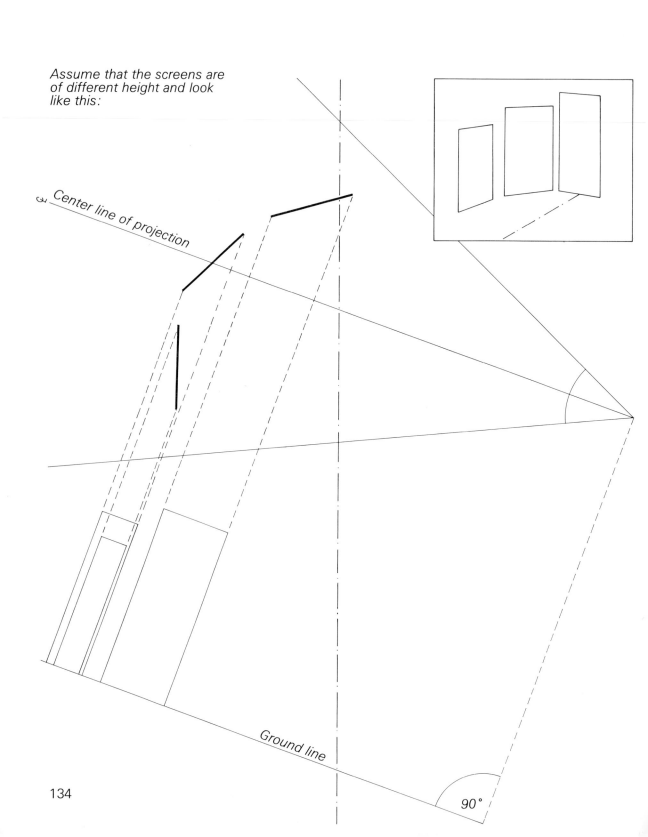

Assume that the screens are
of different height and look
like this:

Center line of projection

Ground line

90°

Finish superimposing the elevation to scale. Now, find the height of the projector. This is decided by several factors. For instance, the higher the luminaire, the nearer the actors can be to the screens without casting shadows on them. However, the placing is usually determined by purely physical factors, such as the heights of bars, or which rostra are actually available for the standing or hanging of projectors. When this is determined, center the screens again in the lens angle, using the same tracing paper as before

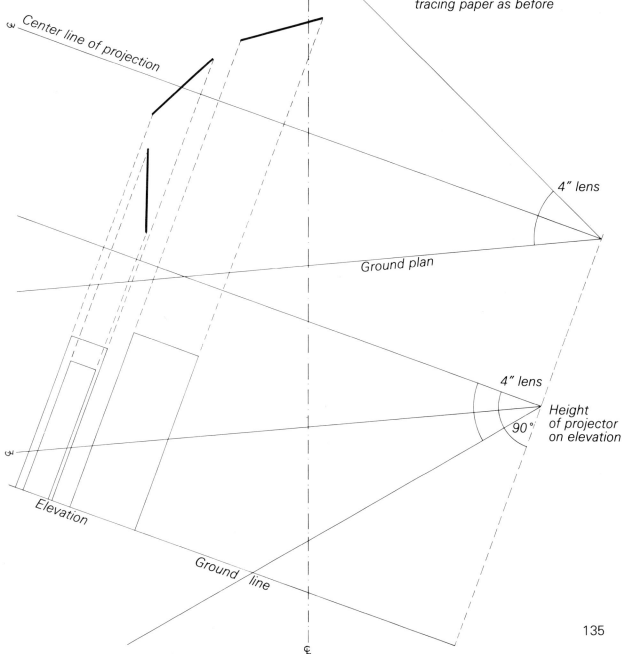

Center line of projection

4″ lens

Ground plan

4″ lens

90°

Height of projector on elevation

Elevation

Ground line

Take the actual dimensions of the slide cartridge of the projector concerned, that is, the dimensions of the particular slide that will project the image. (This varies with the type of projector.) Draw its elevation at 90 degrees to the center line of the elevation projection, at the point where its dimensions coincide with the outside limits of the projection angle

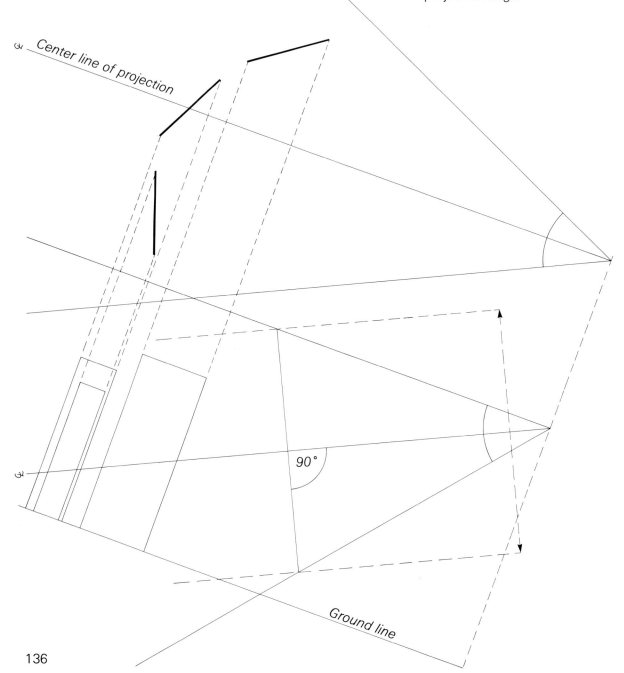

Center line of projection

90°

Ground line

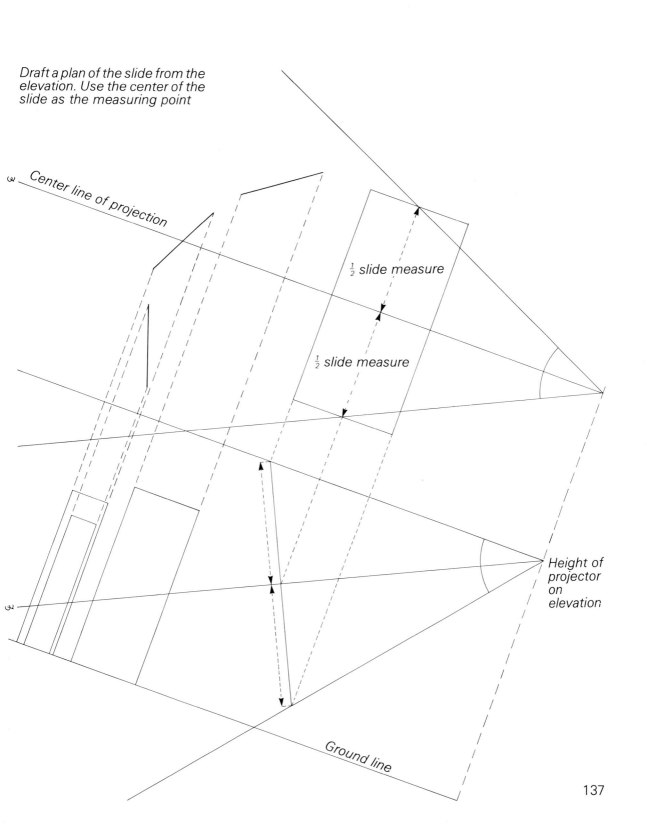

Draft a plan of the slide from the elevation. Use the center of the slide as the measuring point

ω — Center line of projection

$\frac{1}{2}$ slide measure

$\frac{1}{2}$ slide measure

Height of
projector
on
elevation

ω

Ground line

At this point, the drawings are ready to use. Now it will be possible to start working out exactly how to make the slide

Draft lines from all corners of the screens through to the projection point on both plan and elevation. It is helpful to

letter and number the corners, so as to keep track of what is happening. The diagram shows the necessary marking

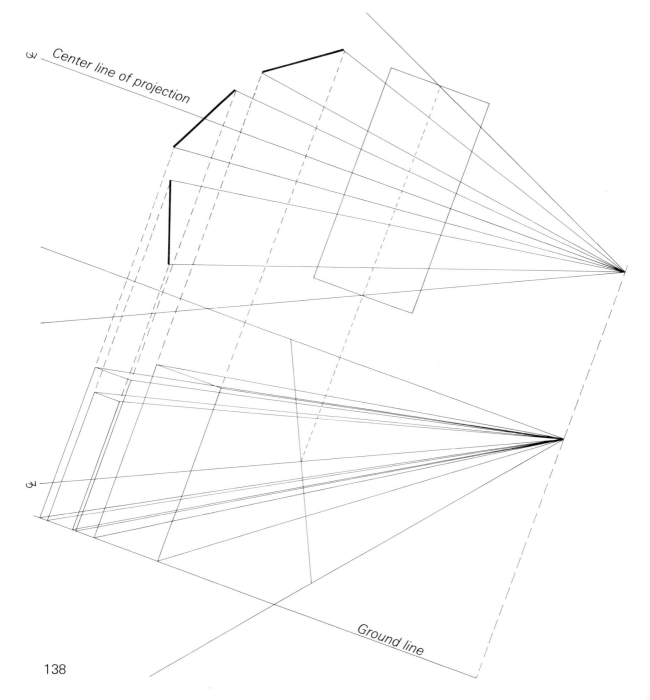

Center line of projection

Ground line

138

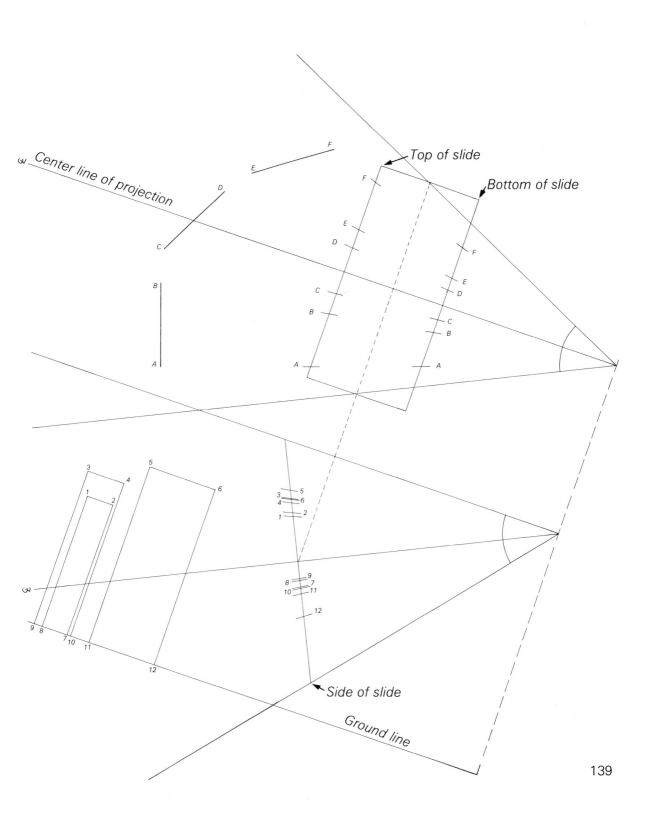

Center line of projection

Top of slide

Bottom of slide

Side of slide

Ground line

139

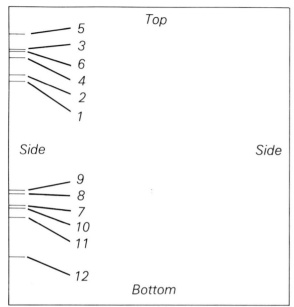

Draw the slide so it is the correct size and enter up the elevation marks on the side

Draft these straight over

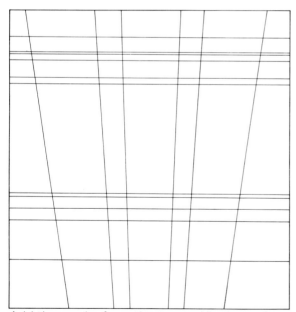

Add the marks from the top and bottom of plan to top and bottom of slide itself and then draft through

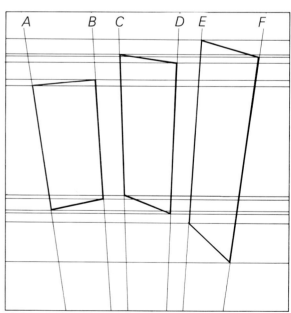

Join up the appropriate co-ordinates to form the image of the three screens on the slide, as shown above

Notes on the use of photographic slides

A wide-angle lens is normally used for projection. Ordinary camera lenses are most unlikely to have a lens of equal width, so the photographer will be unable to place the camera in the exact position on the model that the projector would occupy. Therefore the camera must be moved farther back, to bring the screens into range. Try to match the template with an "enlarger" afterwards. Less distortion occurs if the camera is moved away fom the model horizontally, at the height of the projector, and is kept parallel with the center line of the plan. This method is better than attempting to raise the camera along the center line of the elevation

This is the final drawing, which can be used as a template when painting on to slides or glass. Mask all but the screen areas with "Photo Opaque" paint. Alternatively, it may be used as a template to which photographic transparencies can be matched

Lighting the stage with limited resources

The earlier section in this book on *Lighting the stage* (pages 62-89) dealt mainly with how to light the stage in ideal conditions with a free choice of equipment. More often than not, however, the lighting designer of a small or amateur company may have to be rather more adaptable. The venue is quite likely to have limited resources and a lighting budget that is virtually non-existent. Not only may there be a limited number of luminaires available, but also on the amount of power and the quantity of dimmers that can be used.

Do not despair! There are a number of ways that these restrictions can be overcome or minimized. Very often it is simply a case of using "lateral thinking", looking at the stage concerned with a completely open mind and not necessarily expecting to be able to employ all the conventional equipment in the conventional way. Perhaps a glance through the historical survey (see pages 10-19) might be a very useful undertaking. Earlier lighting experts coped remarkably well without any of our modern engineering and it might be possible to make use of some of their ideas; at the very least, it will serve as a reminder that the situation should never be regarded as impossible.

The particular problems of how to provide both warm and cool washes, sufficient acting-area cover, as well as any color and highlighting required, with what may seem to be inadequate equipment, will be discussed. This chapter explains how to use differing light levels, the versalility of luminaires, cross-plugging, color wheels, and home-made lamps. Admittedly, many more specific difficulties may well need to be overcome, but still the same principles will apply. Exploit whatever is available. Use imagination and initiative. Do experiment with new ideas; and old ones! Be compromized only by the safety of the undertaking. Remember the prime objective is to light the actor. Follow these guidelines and the limited resources may well become stepping stones to greater creativity.

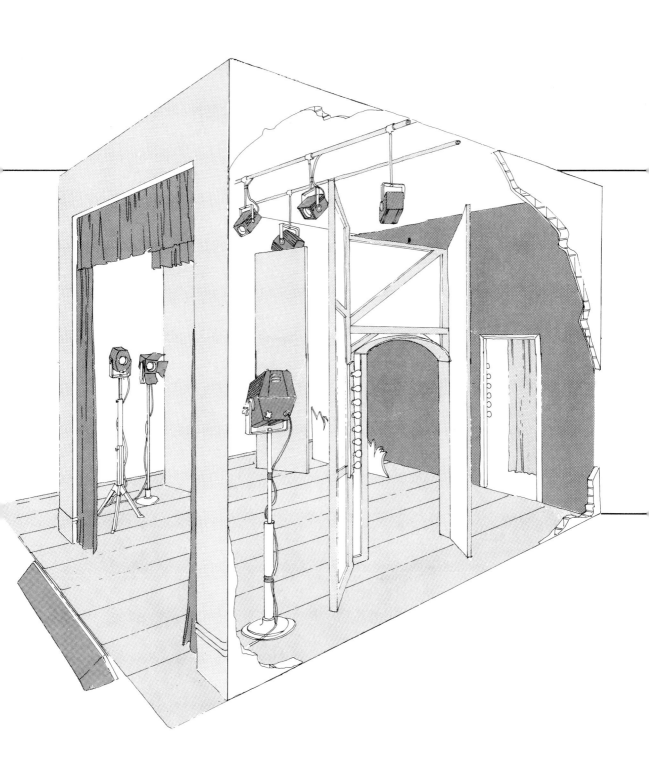

Control and color

Control boards

The most difficult problems to deal with are those presented by a primitive control board. If, for instance, the theater has only a two-scene preset board or, at worst, a single-scene preset board with no group facilities, then the lighting for the show must be designed with this restriction in mind. The director should also be made aware of this limitation very early on because any fast and complicated lighting changes are made virtually impossible, and this must be borne in mind during production and planning.

There are, however, many aspects of limited equipment that, with a little imagination and resourcefulness, can be dealt with and accomodated into the overall scheme.

Providing a warm and cool wash

The lighting designer will generally aim to incorporate a two-color wash. In other words, every luminaire used for front lighting should have a counterpart alongside focused into exactly the same area; this second lamp will be fitted with a different color so that the stage can be given a warm or a cool color wash.

Although this is the ideal situation to achieve, it can prove quite a strain on the available equipment. If a one-color wash only can be used, this will immediately halve the amount of luminaires that will be necessary. It is perfectly acceptable to do this, especially for a one-state show. A day-lit box set could be quite

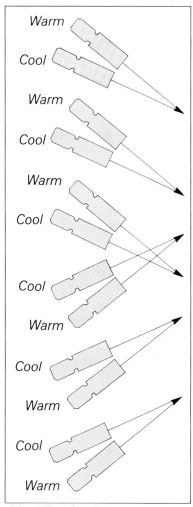

Ideal illumination

adequately covered by a one-color frontlight wash.

The problems occur when this is not acceptable — when the stage must have both a warm and a cool atmosphere. One method of dealing with this situation is described here. First light the acting area in the normal way, but this time use only one luminaire each side to light the same area.

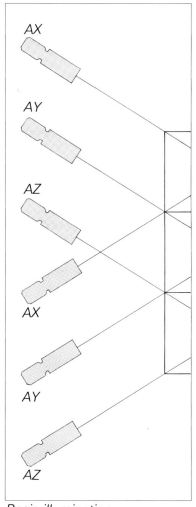

Basic illumination

Use a neutral color for this basic lighting so that the whole stage can be lit quite simply, without any color tones.

Remember that a luminaire with no color is not true white (see page 104), especially at low level. It will probably be nesessary, therefore, to use a color-correction gel to retain the neutral quality of white light. (Try Lee 203 or $\frac{1}{4}$ C.T.)

144

Having achieved this overall neutral cover, the next step is to find a way to light the stage to be both warm and cool.

The desired effect can be achieved by using the front or the back lighting to provide a warm or cool wash. If the designer chooses the front lights to do this, then a wash of the whole stage (in both a warm and a cool wash) will have to be provided by just a few lamps. This is quite feasible — after all,

economy of lamps is exactly what is required in this instance.

If this is the situation, it is useful to remember that you should choose "wash" luminaires which have twice the rated power of the "area" lamps. Thus, if 500 watt area lamps are being used, then choose 1000 watt wash lamps; and if 1000 watt area lamps are being used, then choose 2000 watt wash lamps. On an average stage, it is possible to provide a wash in

this way with only two lamps; one focused stage left of center and the other focused stage right of center. They must be rigged in such a position that the spread of light from the luminaire will cover the whole stage; this may mean using a rather flat angle. Add a color wheel to these two luminaires and the designer will have a choice of five color washes. (There are five color positions on one color wheel.)

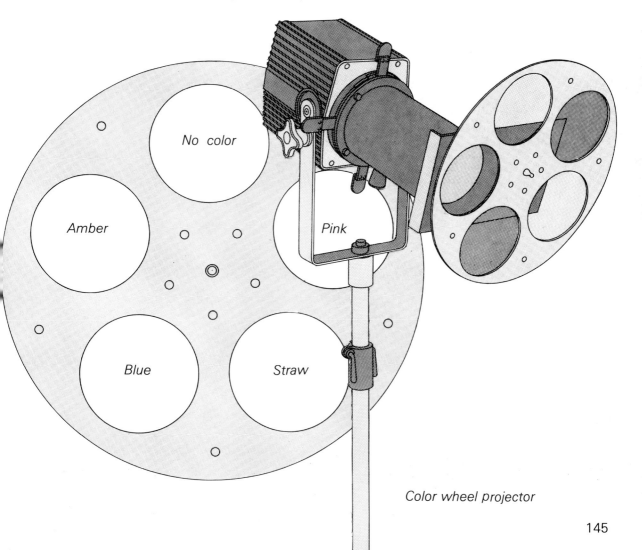

Color wheel projector

Using available resources

Now the designer has the advantage of the whole stage being lit in a controllable way, by use of area-cover luminaires. Moreover, the mood and the temperature of the stage can be altered by means of the colored washes. The diagram below shows a typical frontlight focus plan when using this method of lighting.

It can be quite justifiable to have the colored wash provided by the back lighting rather than the front. This can be particularly useful if any obvious light sources (which may be usefully employed to color the stage) are already coming from the top or from the rear; for example, sunlight or moonlight.

The same principles apply as before. Wash the stage with the chosen color; leave highlighting of actors' faces and special areas to area-color luminaires.

Although this second method of color washing works well in most situations, it may be that, in certain circumstances, it is not sufficiently adaptable.

For example, the designer may be faced with a situation where there must be controllable areas in both a warm and a cool color. Obviously, it would be impossible for moonlight to provide both these colors.

Color wheels

If the dimmers, as well as the lamps, are a limited resource, the designer might then consider using color wheels. One should be fitted to each lamp down one side of the rig and then the neutral-light method can be used on the other side.

It can be seen that color wheels may be "life savers", coming to the rescue in a difficult situation. They are certainly cheaper than hiring the equivalent in extra lamps and dimmers. They can, however, be a problem to set up and synchronize, so the designer must allow sufficient time to do this properly.

A well-organized color-wheel system can overcome many difficulties. On the other hand, if it is not put together correctly, it can lead to hours of frustration and be a total waste of time. So do it properly or not at all!

Using relative light levels

It should be remembered that light levels are relative. For instance, if there is a general luminaire shortage, a bright daytime scene may seem a problem. However, by adjusting

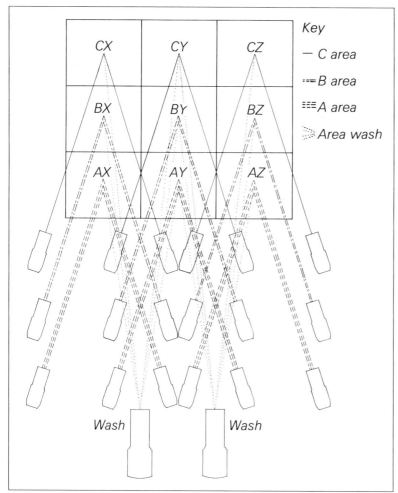

Key

— C area

=== B area

≡≡≡ A area

⫶ Area wash

Cover provided by the wash and acting-area lighting

the eyes of the audience beforehand, the illusion of brightness can be created. Take, for example, a situation where the first scene of a play takes place in full sunlight or needs simply to be seen as a very bright scene. If only a few luminaires are available, ensure that, when the audience walk in, the house lighting is as dim as is practically possible. Under no circumstances should it be bright and glaring. Then, as the houselights go down, try and leave the house in darkness for a moment or two before bringing up the lighting state on the stage. Then the relative brightness of the stage lighting will have far more impact, and the audience really believe they are looking at a brilliantly lit scene — even though the amount of kilowatts lighting the stage may be quite small.

If the bright setting is not in the opening scene but instead follows another scene in the play, then try to avoid high light levels in this preceding scene. If relative light levels are used sensibly, then differentials are always possible, even with small lighting rigs. Sometimes, in theaters which do not impose this type of restriction, a sudden very bright lighting state may be

too much of a shock to the audience's eyes. If this is the case, the lighting state should be brought up, initially, to only 80 per cent and then slowly lifted to full light. Do this gradually, taking a minute or two to effect the change in lighting levels, and then the audience will not detect that this is happening.

"Dead" areas

A designer should always be aware of every inch of the stage which is being used. When lighting with limited resources, it is wise to be aware also of every inch that is not being used. There may well be "dead areas" where a double-cover wash would be a total waste of time; or there may be areas which are used so occasionally that they can be quite adequately lit by a special for just those few moments.

Making the most of the luminaires

Sometimes there may be only unsuitable types or amounts of equipment available. There could, for instance, be far too many profiles and not enough Fresnels; or too many Fresnels and not enough floods. When

this happens, it is often possible for some pieces of equipment to double up for others. It is always worth experimenting with different luminaires to discover their full potential.

For example, if a frosted gel (particularly the new Hamburg variety) is fitted into a profile, it will then give a fairly good soft-edged light, similar to the Fresnel. In the same way, if the lens is removed from a Fresnel, this can convert it into a very plausible floodlight. (Careful use of the barn doors can even transform this into quite a well-controlled light.)

Dimmers

The amount of luminaires may not be the only limiting resource factor for a lighting designer. A lack of dimmers may also be an impediment. With a degree of forethought, this problem can be reduced considerably by either "pairing" (or "cross-plugging") the lamps.

Pairing lamps

Although it is usually desirable to have one lamp per dimmer, it is not always necessary. Lamps lighting the same area or the same piece of set can be paired together to share the same circuit or dimmer. If floods are lighting a cyclorama, these can often be coupled together, perhaps as many as four or five to one circuit, depending on the wattage of the lamps and the loading of the dimmer. Great care should be taken, when pairing up lamps, that the dimmer rating or circuit load is not exceeded. It is also most important to make sure that the correct cable rating is used.

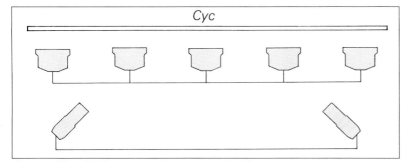

Several luminaires can share one circuit

Cross plugging

A designer will soon realize that not all the luminaires on the rig are necessarily being used in each scene. Therefore it is often possible to cross plug.

This is a system whereby several luminaires, particularly specials, may be able to share the same circuit because they use it at quite different times.

For example, if there is a play with three different acts, it is quite feasible for one circuit to control three different luminaires being used at separate times — provided that cross plugging between the acts is possible. Obviously, all these luminaires must terminate at the plug point of the dimmers and should not "pair" on the bar.

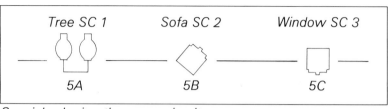

Specials sharing the same circuit

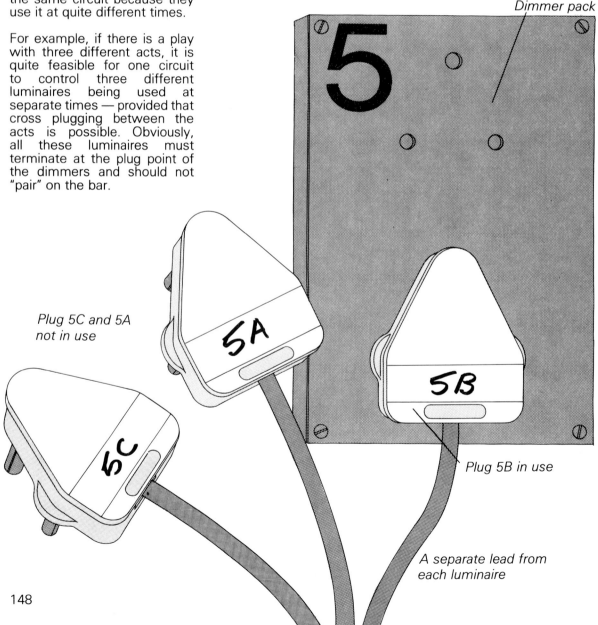

Dimmer pack

Plug 5C and 5A not in use

Plug 5B in use

A separate lead from each luminaire

Home-made luminaires

Using "home-made" luminaires

Another economy is to avoid using upstage luminaires where they are not strictly necessary. When lighting a door backing, or inside a small alcove, for instance, it is a pity to use stage luminaires if they are in short supply. A string or batten of ordinary household bulbs will light a door backing quite efficiently. If a slightly more controllable light source is needed, then it is a good idea to mount the light bulb and holder in a biscuit tin or a clean, large bean can. It is most important to earth the metal can.

It is worth noting that a reflector-type bulb will give even more direction to these "home-made" luminaires. Color gels can, in fact, be cellophane-taped to the front of these makeshift luminaires. Do make sure that there is adequate ventilation by drilling holes in the base of the bean can (or in the top and bottom sides of the biscuit tin). This will stop the casing of the cans becoming unnecessarily hot.

Working within the discipline of limited resources may well be the "norm" for some lighting designers. These designers, and the fortunate ones for whom it is a rare occurrence, will need to use their ingenuity and experience to deal with the difficulties that arise. Hopefully, the ideas in this chapter will help solve some of the problems. At all times, have a regard for the safety of any measures taken and then fulfil all the aims of the lighting designer as best you can — within the particular restraints imposed.

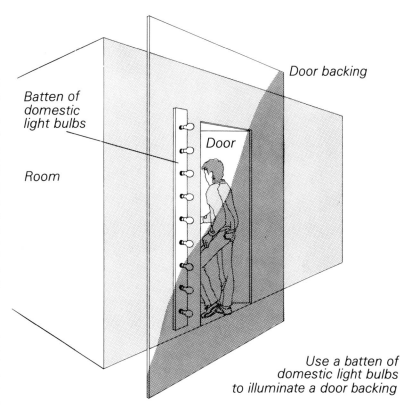

Door backing

Batten of domestic light bulbs

Door

Room

Use a batten of domestic light bulbs to illuminate a door backing

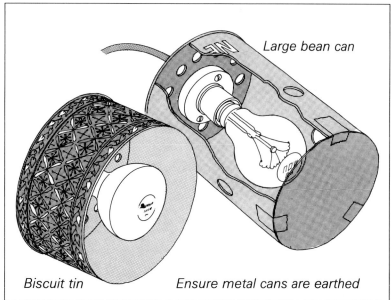

Large bean can

Biscuit tin

Ensure metal cans are earthed

A home-made luminaire can be made from a bean can or from a biscuit (cookie) tin

Basic electrical theory and safety

The handling and installation of lighting equipment should never be undertaken without knowledge of the electrical principles involved. This chapter explains basic electrical theory and how to keep well within the bounds of safety. Unless the lighting mechanic is a practised electrician, professional advice will be essential. Do not ever attempt to "work in the dark" or you may end up doing just that!

Electricity consists of charged particles called electrons which exist in every kind of matter.

Electrons are pumped through conductors by a generator or battery. This generator exerts pressure, which is measured in volts, on the electrons.

An electrical circuit can be likened in many ways to a pumped water system. For instance, the greater the force a pump exerts on the water in a system, the greater the water flow (measured in gallons per minute). The greater the force exerted by a generator or a battery on the electrons, the greater the electron flow will be (measured in amps and called the current).

In a water system, changing the size of the pipework affects the water flow. A wider pipe will allow more water to flow through, in a given time, than a narrower pipe of the same length. This is because the narrow pipe resists the flow more than a wide one. Similarly, electron flow can be affected by the size and type of material that the electrons pass through.

This is called resistance and is measured in ohms. Resistance is defined as the ratio between the electron pressure (volts) and the electron flow (amps).

The formula for resistance is:
$$\text{Resistance (R)} = \frac{\text{volts (V)}}{\text{amps (I)}}$$

The symbol for resistance is R (measured in ohms). The symbol for electron pressure is V (measured in volts), and the symbol for electron flow is I (measured in amps). This knowledge may be useful for later calculations.

◇Electricity

Making and using electrical energy

Electrons must complete a circuit in order to flow. Every battery or generator has two terminals and if a wire is connected between these, electrons will then flow from one to the other. The terminals are labeled + (positive) and — (negative), as shown below.

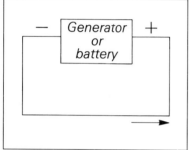

A simple circuit

Energy is given to the electrons in an electrical circuit by pumping them from a low voltage to a high voltage. Energy is released by letting electrons fall from a high voltage to a low voltage.

Whenever the electrons flow from a higher to a lower voltage (through a piece of wire, a motor, or some other electrical apparatus), their energy is transferred to the equipment. If the energy is not recovered, by using it for mechanical work for instance, it simply heats up the wire or device.

So the circuit in the diagram above will allow electrons to flow but the energy generated will be entirely wasted in a form of heat. This is caused by the resistance of the wire, rather like friction might produce heat.

By inserting a device that utilizes the electrical energy in the circuit, we can make the energy work for us.

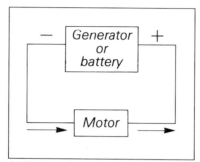

Utilizing electrical energy

Alternating current

So far we have considered current flowing in one direction only. This is called "direct current" or DC. Alternating current circuits work just like the DC type, except that the current is first travelling in one direction and then in the other. The current will literally alternate above (positive) and below (negative), zero amps, making one complete cycle.

The frequency of alternating current is measured in hertz. One hertz equals one cycle per second. Electricity supplied to industry and for domestic use consists of alternating current at a frequency of 50 hertz in the UK and 60 hertz in the USA.

How electrical energy is controlled

There are only two ways electrical energy can be controlled. The first is simply to control the amount of energy that is put into a circuit by the battery or generator. However, this is not always possible. The voltage of a mains supply, for instance, is constant.

The second way is to regulate the energy, using variable resistance to "throttle" the electricity supply. In practical terms, this means that electrical energy can be controlled only by switching on and off, or by regulation.

The mains electrical supply

The electricity generated at power stations is normally in the form of a four-wire system (three phases and one neutral).

There are three coils inside the generator. One end of each coil is connected to a common point called the neutral. The other end of each coil remains separate and is called live. The coils are spaced equally around the generator at 120 degrees — this provides a "phase angle" (between voltages) of 120 degrees. Because of the phase angle, the three phases, or

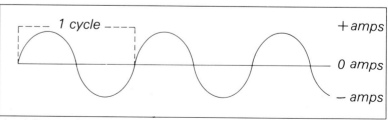

An AC waveform

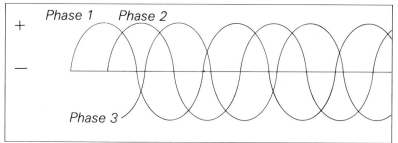

A three-phase AC waveform

Fuses

A fuse is simply a weak link in an electrical circuit — a piece of wire that will heat up and melt, should excess current pass through it. A fuse is designed to melt before the rest of the circuit is damaged. The current at which this occurs is known as its rating.

waveforms, reach their peak voltage at different times.

The electricity produced at the power station is transformed up to a very high voltage and then distributed. At substations the voltage is transformed down to the mains (local) level. Substation transformers have three coils, which have their respective neutrals connected together. This neutral point is connected to an earth electrode which is buried in the ground.

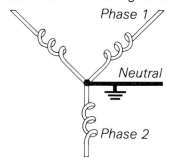

A three-phase transformer used in a substation

Between any two phases there will be a voltage present which is equal to the sum of the voltage at each of the phases. Between any phase and neutral there is a voltage equal to the mains (local) supply. In the UK, these voltages are 415 volts between phases, and 240 volts between any phase and neutral

(USA equivalents 208:120). The three-phase and neutral supply is then separated down to feed houses and so on. One phase might feed a road of houses and the next phase might feed another road. If large supply requirements are needed, such as for heavy industry or for theaters, the three-phase and neutral systems can be fed directly into one building and the apparatus within can be split across the phases. The Theatre Royal, in Bristol, England, has an 800 amp per phase, three-phase and neutral supply. This is necessary as there is a dimmer capability alone of 510 kw (equal to 2140 amps).

Earthing (ground)

At the consumer end of the electricity supply, exposed metal parts of apparatus, and also the water and gas pipes, are wired to the ground via another earth electrode. This ensures that should a fault occur in the apparatus or wiring, electricity can travel through the electrode back to the earth at the substation. It will immediately cause a dead short and blow the fuse protecting the apparatus. This makes sure that the faulty equipment is disconnected from the supply for obvious safety reasons.

Every phase (live) wire or conductor in an electrical installation must be protected against excess current by a fuse. The rating of this fuse should not exceed the lowest rated conductor in the circuit being protected. What this means, in simple terms, is that to protect a piece of cable rated at 10 amps, a 10 amp fuse must be inserted between the cable and the supply, and so on.

Fuses must always be inserted in the live side of a circuit, as should any switch, because the live wire is the potentially dangerous one. It can give an electric shock or start a fire, if a fault should occur.

When replacing any blown fuse, the replacement must be of the same voltage, current rating, and type as the original fuse (see also page 154). Then it will continue to provide the same measure of excess current protection.

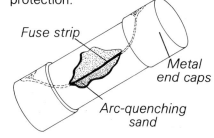

Cut-away of a fuse

153

Safety

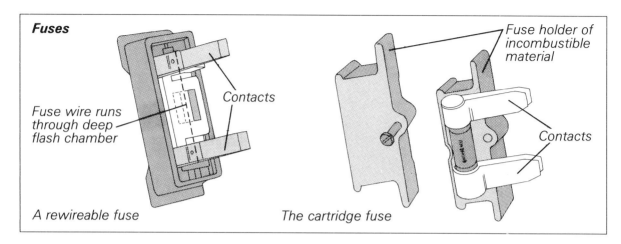

Fuses

Contacts

Fuse wire runs
through deep
flash chamber

A rewireable fuse

Fuse holder of
incombustible
material

Contacts

The cartridge fuse

Cables

When replacing any blown fuse, the replacement must be of the same voltage, current rating, and type as the original fuse (see page 153). Then it will continue to provide exactly the same measure of excess-current protection.

Most of the cables that are used in a theater by the lighting crew or department will be for only temporary lighting installations that will last just for the duration of the show concerned.

Therefore the cables will be constantly mobile and must be very durable and flexible, in order to take the strain.

They must be of an approved type for safety reasons and of the correct gauge to carry the necessary current.

Stranded wire, which is made up of small wires grouped together to form a single conductor, is the most flexible and therefore the best to use. Solid wire is normally used only for permanent installations.

Small voltage twin-core cable is very useful for the wiring up of telephone bells, alarms, or perhaps a front-door buzzer.

All cables should be regularly checked and serviced. Always keep an eye open for any cracks in the insulation, which could well make the cable potentially dangerous. ◇

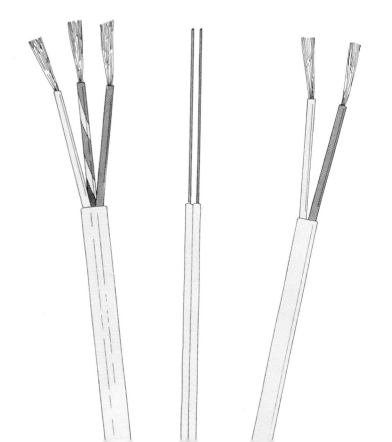

Circuit breakers

A circuit breaker is a current-sensitive switch which will "trip" with any current overload, but which can be reset afterwards.

It is extremely unwise to repair a fuse that has blown (or a breaker which has tripped) without first finding out why this has happened. It is quite likely that the fault still exists. For example, if a short circuit has occurred between the two conductors of a flexible cord, then their insulation may have melted. The conductors will therefore be exposed to touch and could cause a shock if the fuse is replaced.

The fault should be repaired immediately, or the apparatus temporarily disconnected for repair, before replacing the fuse that has blown.

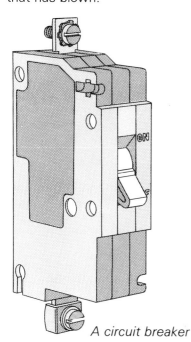

A circuit breaker

Calculating current

It is very important to know how to calculate the amount of current a device uses. This knowledge is important for two main reasons:

1 So that you can be sure that the electricity supply is capable of feeding the device with the required power.

2 So that you ensure that the cable feeding the device is able to take the necessary load.

As theater lighting rigs tend to be temporary, many link cables are used to connect luminaires to their dimmers. These cables must not carry more than their recommended load, otherwise overheating could easily occur. This could result in either a fuse blowing or, worse still, a fire breaking out.

The first thing to do is to find out what size cable is being used. Then check its current-carrying capabilities. (This can be taken from the IEE Regulations in the UK and from the National Electric Code article — which is part of the National Fire Code — in the USA.)

Finally, the luminaire loading for each cable can be calculated, by using the formula below:

I (current in amps) = $\frac{watts}{volts}$

For example, with a 1000 watt luminaire on a 120 volt supply, the luminaire would require a current of just over 8 amps; as shown in the formula below:

$$I = \frac{1000 \text{ (watts)}}{120 \text{ (volts)}} = 8.3 \text{ amps}$$

Thus, the cable used to feed power safely to the 1000 watt luminaire would need a capacity of about 9 amps.

How many luminaires?

The formula used above can be used to calculate the number of luminaires that may be fed from a mains supply of known capacity. If the mains supply is, for instance, 120 volts at 60 amps, the following is true:

mains capacity in watts
= 120 x 60
= 7200 watts

Thus it can be seen that a maximum of seven 1000 watt luminaires may be safely supplied.

Safety

Always electrically isolate any electrical device when attending to it.

Do not plug a luminaire into a hot (live) circuit.

Do not switch dimmers on or off unless all luminaires are faded to "Off".

Do not allow beverages near the control boards, dimmers, or patch panels.

Only a qualified electrician should connect a portable dimming system to the electrical service.

Keep luminaires away from draperies etc.

Check all color frames are securely inserted.

Series and parallel wiring

Series

In series wiring, the total current passes through every appliance in the circuit.

If one lamp or appliance is used in the circuit, its voltage must match that of the supply. By placing another lamp of the same rating in series with the first, the voltage is equally divided between the two, (as shown in the second diagram).

Each 110 volt lamp is now only half as bright as it would be if it were the only lamp in the circuit. This is because it now receives only half its rated voltage.

For the two lamps in series to run at the correct brightness, they would need to have a voltage rating of 55 volts.

In this way, it is possible to use low-voltage lamps on a mains circuit. The voltage rating of the lamp must be divided into the mains-supply voltage in order to determine the number of lamps to use. This is how most sets of Christmas-tree lights are wired.

The drawback with this method is that only one lamp needs to "blow" and the entire set of lamps is put out of action.

Finding the faulty lamp can be quite a long process, especially if there are a large number within the circuit.

Parallel

With a parallel wiring system, the total current is divided between several appliances (fixtures) individually connected across the supply.

The voltage of each appliance must be equal to that of the supply. However, if one lamp in this circuit should fail, the others will not be affected. This is how electricity is normally distributed from the power station to domestic appliances.

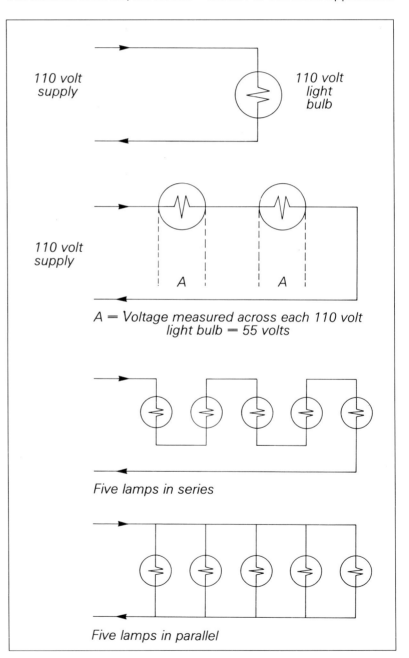

A = Voltage measured across each 110 volt light bulb = 55 volts

Five lamps in series

Five lamps in parallel

Transformers

Transformers are the devices used to change one alternating current voltage to another. They consist of an iron core around which there are two windings. One winding might have, for instance, 2000 turns and the other, 1000 turns. If the 2000 turn winding (the primary winding) is connected to an AC supply, then a voltage will also be generated on the 1000 turn winding (the secondary winding). This voltage will be half of the voltage connected to the primary winding.

The output voltage of the transformer will depend upon the ratio of the number of turns in each winding.

In the example, the voltage was stepped down, but by reversing the turns ratio, the voltage can be stepped up instead.

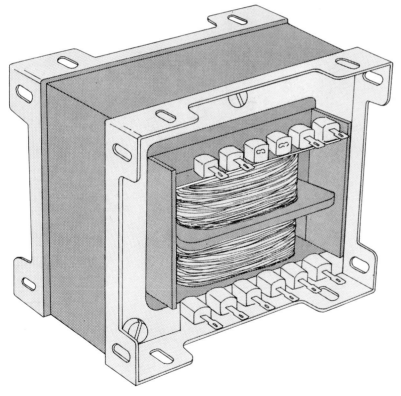

A transformer

Precautions

It is essential when carrying out any electrical maintenance or wiring to remember at all times that a potentially lethal form of energy is being used. However, if the work is undertaken with a sense of responsibility and the correct materials are used, then a safe repair or installation will be successfully achieved.

The safety of all electrical appliances and wiring can be ensured in three ways:

1 Insulation

Phase terminals or any other equipment should always be covered in such a way that no-one can touch any live parts.

2 Earthing (ground)

Metal casings, or any exposed metal of an appliance, should be electrically connected to earth (ground) to ensure safe use.

3 Protection against fire risk

Always use cable that can carry the required current loading. Protect the circuits with the correct sizes and types of fuses or circuit breakers.

If the principles in this chapter are always carefully observed and the lighting equipment is regularly checked, then you, and the theater you are working in, should remain intact. It is beyond the scope of this book to explore the subject in greater detail but there are many other books available on electrical theory and practice. When working in this field, ignorance is not bliss!

Lighting productions by John A. Williams

Lighting designers can only successfully develop their art by applying all their ideas in a practical, theater situation. The professional, as well as the amateur, is learning all the time, forever gaining knowledge with experience.

The accumulation of skills is a gradual process but this chapter of the book allows us to tap the knowledge of the expert, as it explores some of the problems and interesting productions that John A. Williams has met in his role as a lighting designer, overseeing a hundred and twenty productions, to date.

We learn just how particular difficulties of some productions were overcome; the way the lighting was approached; and how equipment and techniques can be applied to highlight creatively the special qualities of each piece of theater.

Four plays come under scrutiny: *A Midsummer Night's Dream, The Recruiting Officer, When the Wind Blows,* and *Oh What a Lovely War!*

In each case, the complexities of the lighting can be easily understood and are particularly relevant to the theories already explored in the book.

These productions are all quite different. Not only are the plays dissimilar but the style of production and staging take quite different forms, so many varying lighting techniques are demonstrated. It is hoped that even the larger rigs can be appreciated and will be of help, even to the beginner. (Far more complex lighting designs are demonstrated in other books but have no place within the context of the *"Create Your Own..."* series.)

It is particularly interesting to note that the stimulation of trying to solve the specific complications of each play seems to bring the greatest satisfaction and success. The resolving of problems "in the field" is the best experience available. Through this chapter we see just how this is done.

WHEN THE WIND BLOWS

A Midsummer Night's Dream

William Shakespeare

The Recruiting Officer

OH WHAT A LOVELY WAR!

...atefully acknowledges
...ouncil of Great Britain,
...unty of Avone

form, would have prevented any type of masked, low cross light. Together, the set designer and lighting designer overcame the problem by "tenting" the cyclorama.

When this method is used, the bottom section of the "cyc" (cyclorama) is actually split in several places, in a line from the stage to about the midway point of the cyc's drop (in this particular case, at about four meters from the stage floor).

Then, if the upstage edge of the "tent" is pulled off stage and the downstage edge is pulled on stage, a hidden space is created between these two edges where a boom of light can be successfully masked.

This method of incorporating cross-light positions in a seemingly impossible situation worked very well. Apart from a slight billowing effect, the audience really had no means of detecting that the cyclorama had been split in this way.

The second major task was to transform the "cyc" area from a very deep-blue night color to daylight. As the majority of the play takes place at night, the prime use of the cyclorama was to create the illusion of the vast, deep sky at this mystical time.

We decided that, rather than use a white cyclorama and then light it deep-blue, we would use a royal-blue cyclorama. The problem with lighting a white cyclorama to create the blue sky at night is that the cyclorama will "glow" blue, and we needed instead to give an impression of great "depth". Also, when lighting is used in this way, it

Richard Cottrell's production of *A Midsummer Night's Dream* at the Bristol Old Vic presented the production team with several technically demanding requirements.

The set design, conceived by Bob Crowley, incorporated a wrap-around cyclorama which enveloped three sides of the staging area all the way from

the floor to the flies. It was decided very early, in fact pre-production, that some of the sequences the director had in mind would work only with the use of low cross light — a light that would travel from one side of the stage to the other, illuminating the actors and nothing else.

The most obvious problem was the one presented by the wrap-around cyclorama. This structure, in its initial shape and tends to pick up stray and reflected light from the stage. Having procured a deep-blue cyclorama, the only remaining difficulty now was finding a way to turn this deep-blue night sky into the color of daylight when required. It is a simple matter to light color into a sheet of white material but far more difficult to "light it out". As it happened, it had already been planned to use a second surround in front of the cyclorama, so it was decided to utilize this medium to overcome the problem. This second surround was a wrap-around, wide-mesh gauze, which followed the line of the cyclorama. It ran a meter or so away from the upstage section of the cyclorama and then closed up to lie just a few inches away from it down the sides.

On to this wide-mesh gauze were attached hundreds of calico leaves. For the majority of the time these leaves would remain unlit and be simply silhouetted against the blue cyclorama. The floods were placed between the cyclorama and the gauze. (The gauze was drawn away from the top of the cyclorama down the side of the stage to allow for this.)

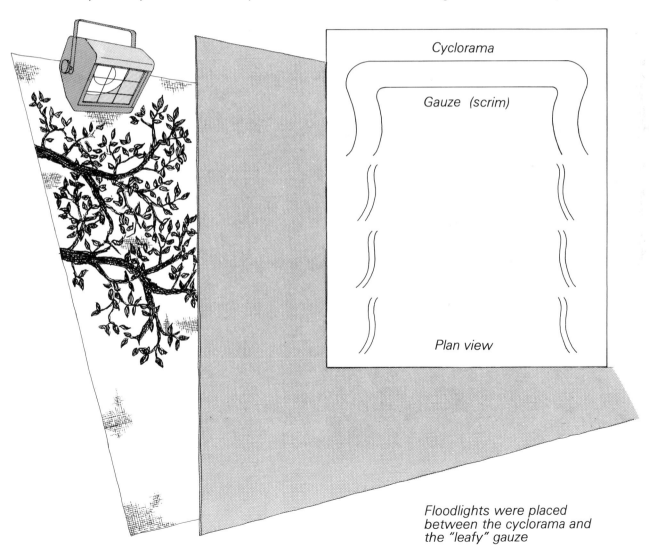

Cyclorama

Gauze (scrim)

Plan view

Floodlights were placed between the cyclorama and the "leafy" gauze

161

A Midsummer Night's Dream

The idea was that, as daylight dawned, the leaves would be lit in a progression of colors until full daylight was reached, and the dark-blue cyclorama beyond quite forgotten. It worked "like a dream"!

The third problem was to find a means of accomplishing the director's vision of the opening sequence in the woods. The technical difficulties were, in fact, two-fold.

First it was decided that the wood should be revealed as moving spangles of light through trees.

Secondly, Puck was then to appear, in a stylized way, dancing around on the upstage portion of the set.

To settle the first requirement, a cheap "moving light through trees" effect was needed. This was achieved by the use of three projectors which were fitted with metal slides of leaf cut-outs. Placed in front of the projectors was a continuously rotating color wheel. This had been fitted not with color, but with metal strips fixed into the color holes.

A smoke effect was billowed into the woods to create an eerie mist. Then the broken rays of light from the projectors with the leaf slides imitated the dance of light through trees.

The rotating color wheel in front of the projectors motivated the individual lines of light, so that they produced a constantly changing effect.

The second problem imposed by the opening scene was how

to light Puck, who was up stage, in an "interesting or unusual manner" (director's quote).

Unfortunately cross light was impracticable — because the "tenting" did not start until farther down the stage.

Front light was considered too boring, and top or back light would not really reveal the character sufficiently to the audience.

So it would appear that bottom light was the only answer. Fortunately the acting area had been designed as a rake, a raised area of stage which sloped to the normal stage level at the sides and front.

It was therefore possible to conceal luminaires in the upstage portion of the rake. Puck could then stand over each of the luminaires in turn, to be lit in an "interesting and unusual manner", and at the same time, his appearance would be such that the audience would instantly recognize him.

Having discovered ways around the specific problems raised by this production, general decisions now had to be taken.

So much of the stage was being used at any one time, I chose to light the production in what might be termed as area lighting (both from the front, side, and back) with a good number of "specials" thrown in.

The area-lighting rig used was symmetrical, that is to say, the equipment allocation could be seen as a mirror image each side of the center line, although all the colors chosen were

not necessarily symmetrically placed. The stage was divided into a grid of twelve sections, and lit as shown on the right.

Each section was front lit, to as near a 45 degree convention as the theater would allow. Four lights were focused into each area. Two warm colors, (a number 3 from stage right, and a number 73 from stage left) and two cool colors (a number 61 on each side).

The overall light was made up to full by three colors rigged on each side — a medium-grade blue (a number 45 from stage right and a number 40 from stage left), a golden amber-straw (a number 98 on each side) and a light blue (a number 69 on each side).

There was also a wash of apricot (number 47) and a back-light wash of deep blue (number 119), used mainly just to color the stage, as the sculpturing was left to the cross light.

The lighting for the whole stage area was very controllable within each section. So much so that one section could be lit in a relatively "normal" manner, while another section could be lit in a stylized manner, by using a cross light.

Thus, each section was able to take on a different individual quality, and yet, quite important for this production, could also appear to be exactly the same as another, when necessary.

This form of area lighting is not always favored, but it can work very well with open staging and was certainly most successful on this occasion.

Area plan of color wash

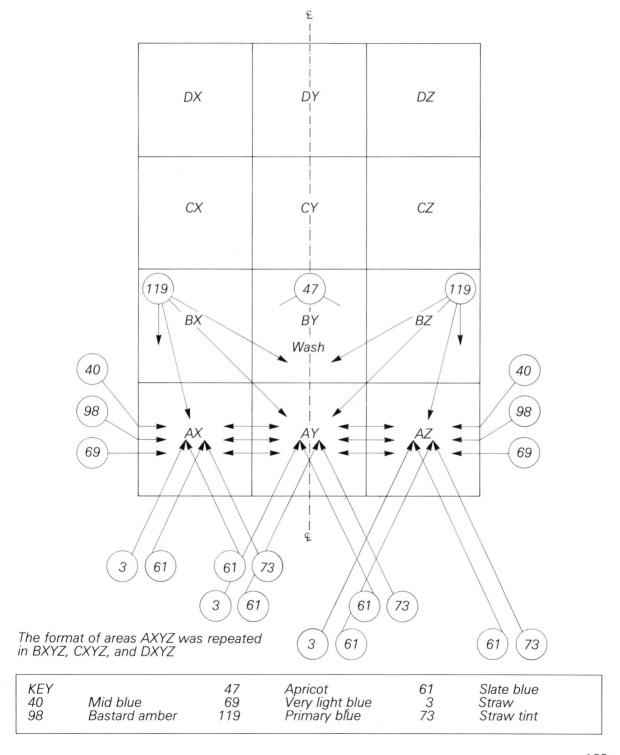

The format of areas AXYZ was repeated
in BXYZ, CXYZ, and DXYZ

KEY		47	Apricot	61	Slate blue
40	Mid blue	69	Very light blue	3	Straw
98	Bastard amber	119	Primary blue	73	Straw tint

Lighting plan

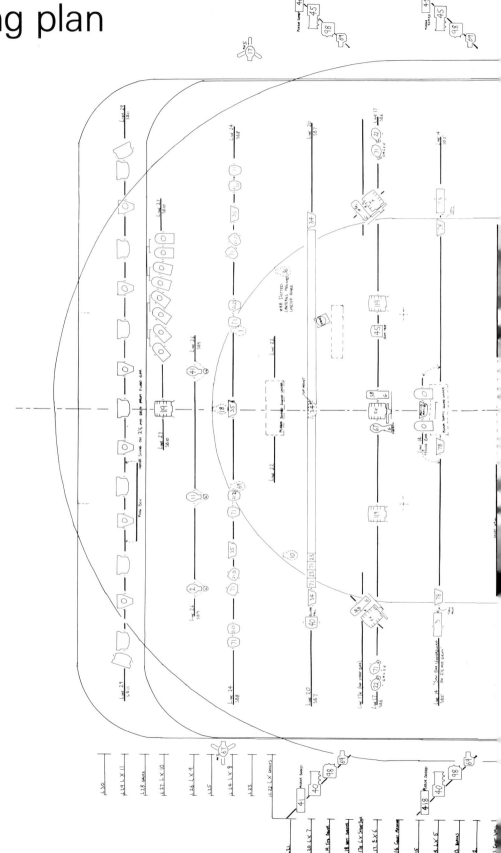

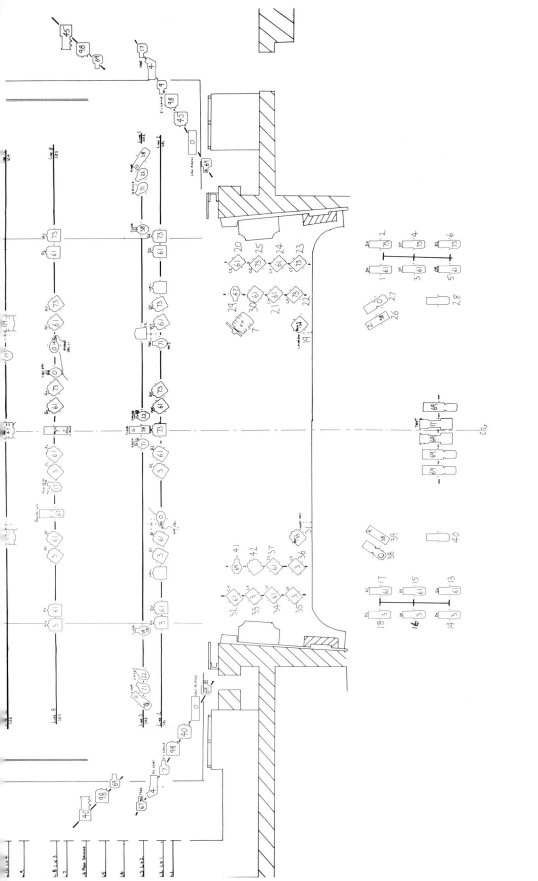

165

Adrian Noble's production of *The Recruiting Officer* was first performed at the Opera House in Buxton and subsequently at the Theatre Royal in Bristol, England. However, it is the production at the Assembly Hall in Edinburgh, Scotland, for the 1979 Edinburgh Festival, which is the most interesting one to examine from the lighting point of view.

To all intents and purposes, the play was lit in the round (or arena). Moreover, the show was also running concurrently with *Troilus and Cressida*, another Bristol Old Vic production. As these two plays were part of a repertoire, the two lighting rigs had to be successfully "married".

Another designer, Francis Reid, was in charge of the lighting for *Troilus and Cressida* so it was necessary for the two designers to co-operate on the project.

Together we designed a rig of such versatility that the only change necessary between the two shows was the switch of colors on eight Par blazers. This simplicity was vitally important as there was very little time available between the two plays — so refocusing or repatching had to be avoided at all costs.

Before proceeding with an explanation of the rig, a description of the set will be helpful. Although both plays used more or less the same

acting areas, the upstage sections of each were, to say the least, incompatible.

Troilus and Cressida had a drawbridge-type of staircase leading up to an upper level. This staircase was sandwiched between two towers. For *The Recruiting Officer*, the set designer, Bob Crawley, used a sky-cloth, which was inclined over the acting area at an angle of about 25 degrees, thus effectively masking the staircase and towers.

The principle acting area for both plays was a raked stage measuring 6.5 meters by 7.5 meters, with the audience on three sides. It was decided to use a nine-segment format for this; three up and three across. A "normal" two-color wash was required (one warm and one cool) and, if possible, it was hoped to light each section from all four sides (that is at 90 degrees separation).

1kw Fresnels could have been used here, as sharp-edge focusing on the acting area was not required. Unfortunately, a quick calculation revealed that there would not be enough equipment to light each section by this method — at any rate, no lights would be left over for specials and other remaining requirements: so "Plan Two" went into operation.

As previously described in this book (see pages 87-89), there are basically two ways of lighting an acting area in the round or a thrust stage. Either four lamps can be used at 90 degrees; or three lamps at 120 degrees (doubling this if a two-color wash is needed). Obviously, the first method gives a smoother, finished effect. It is also easier to use the lights and to "pair" them. The second method is, however, quite adequate. Both designers felt that the central areas in both shows (CY and BY) were definitely strong focus areas. It was therefore decided that these areas would be lit by 90 degrees separation and that the perimeter areas (AX, AY, AZ, BX, BZ, CX, and CZ) would be lit by 120 degrees separation.

Another unusual problem raised by the design was that the center part of the acting area (CY and BY) was wider than the perimeter areas. So the area CY was lit by the format shown in diagram 1.

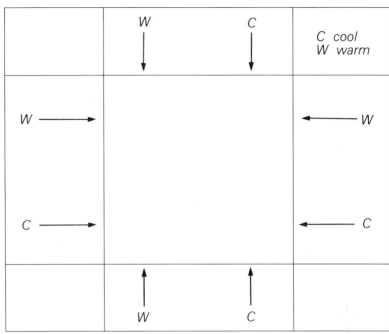

1 Ideal method of lighting each section

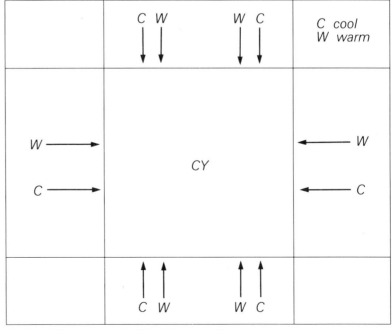

2 Possible method of lighting a wider area

The Recruiting Officer

Because lights could not be rigged directly behind area BY, the format shown in diagram 3 was used for this section:

The other perimeter sections were lit by the rather more conventional method, using 120 degree separation.

To allow flexibility of control, each angle had its own dimmer. The lighting of the basic nine areas needed thirty dimmers and, with the doubling up required by the two-color wash, the overall plan demanded sixty dimmers and channels. The final arrangement, shown in diagramatic form, is on the opposite page (diagram 5).

Having decided on the area cover, a mutual choice of color was needed for the area wash. The cool wash was no problem. Both designers wanted a fairly substantial blue because, as well as cooling the lighting states, there were some long night scenes to be catered for. Therefore Cinemoid 61 (slate blue) was mutually acceptable.

However, the color for the warm wash was slightly more difficult to arrange. Most of the "warm" states in *The Recruiting Officer* were to be exteriors. Therefore it would obviously be preferable if pinks could be avoided, and colors from the straw range chosen, such as straw (number 3), straw tint (number 73), or no-color straw (Rosco 804). Perhaps even open-white would work?

Troilus and Cressida, on the other hand, included a large number of interior states, and a set that, on occasion, would benefit from some pink toning.

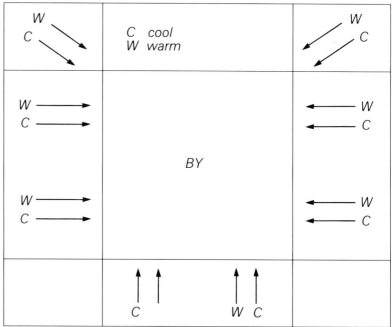

3 This section could be lit from the front and sides only

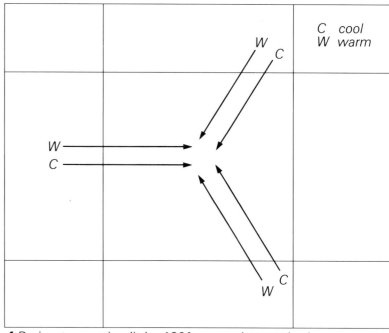

4 Perimeter section lit by 120° separation method

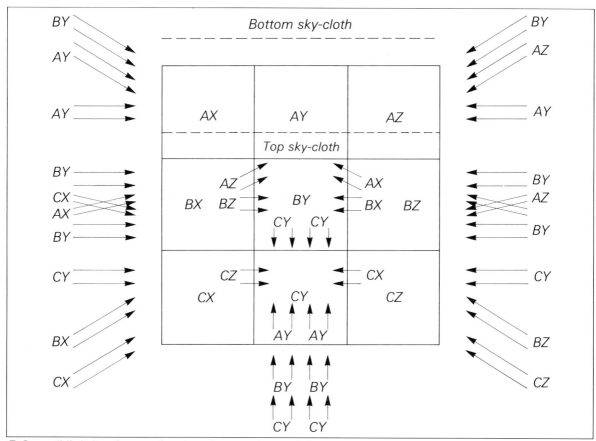

5 *Overall lighting format for the nine sections of the stage*

The "pros and cons" of all the tints in the pink and straw range were discussed at length. Eventually, it was decided that a straw would be the most mutually beneficial color wash, providing that it was not too deep a tint. So a "no-color-straw" (Rosco 804) was the final compromise. Pink toning was obtained for *Troilus and Cressida* by adding some pink downlight wash (number 52).

The sky-cloth for *The Recruiting Officer* was lit with ten 1 kw linear T/H (tungsten/halogen) floods. Five 252 projectors

provided clouds, stars, a rainbow, and forked lightning. Because of the angle of the sky-cloth, the projectors had to be dropped 1.5 meters from the main lighting grid to lessen distortion; and, as seen from the plan, they had to be sited at the far end of the rig to prevent shadows being created by the other luminaires.

Each show, of course, used its own specials, which were occasionally borrowed by the other production. For example, there were sixteen Patt 23s with "break-up" gobos, which

were used to texture the upper set on *Troilus and Cressida*. Used at a low level, these gobo effects were also very helpful in *The Recruiting Officer*, when they served to relieve the monotony of the plain sky-cloth.

Thus the limitations imposed by the in-the-round staging and the sharing of the lighting rig were all overcome successfully and, in fact, utilized to very good effect. Working within quite strict disciplines can actually fire the creative spirit — so do not be daunted by a seemingly impossible situation.

Lighting plan

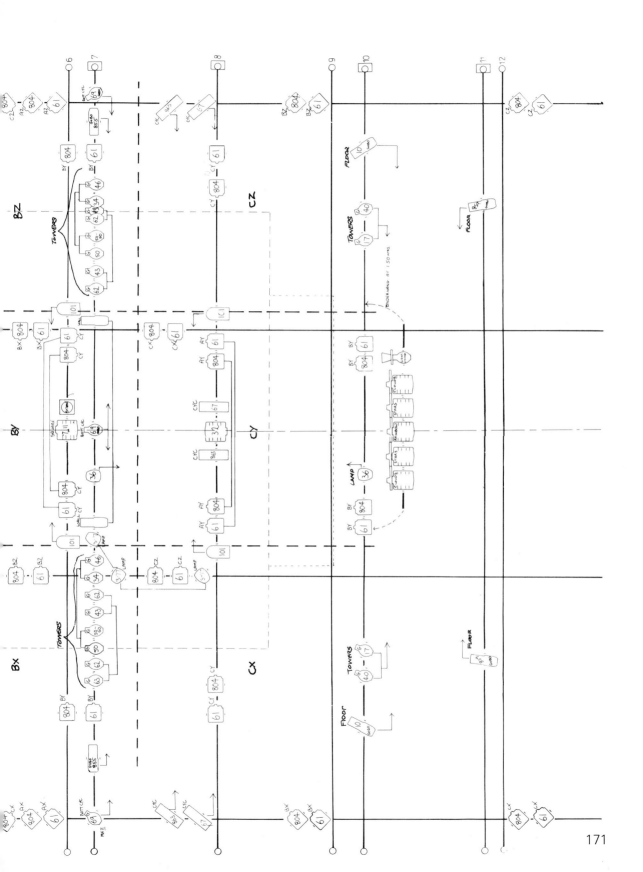

171

WHEN THE WIND BLOWS

Illustration © Raymond Briggs

When the Wind Blows was one of the most evocative theatrical pieces it has ever been my experience to light. It was also one of the most exciting, claiming much critical acclaim for its special effects when it opened in the West End. Credit for these effects must be shared with Dave Bryant (production electrician) and Nick Jones (sound designer). A brief description of the play's content may help to illustrate the special problems involved in lighting this production.

The play is focused on the experience of two of the most famous characters created by the author, Raymond Briggs. These are Gentleman Jim and his wife, Hilda, who live in an idyllic little home in the country. Here they face together the horrors of a nuclear attack and the subsequent after-effects.

During the holocaust they receive no immediate injuries except minor burns but, as the play progresses, they slowly die from the effects of radiation. Hilda's naïveté throughout their plight underlines the sheer terror of such an event.

The broad outline of the lighting requirements was planned so that it would follow and amplify the degradation of life after the explosion.

Therefore it would begin with a bright and sunny, cheerful summer's afternoon. The designer, Billy Meal, had created a simple but very effective set. This featured a bungalow on stage with, as it were, the front wall removed.

A path led around the bungalow and also enclosed a small front garden. A cyclorama encircled the set, with a tree and a telegraph pole set in front.

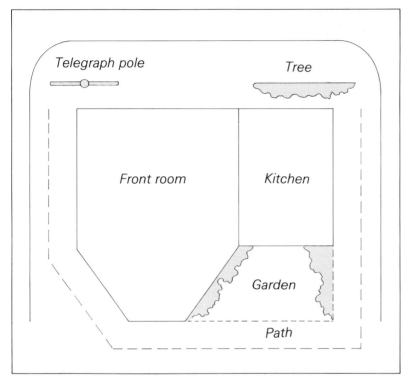

Plan of the set

Fairly strict area separation was required. Each of several "units" needed to be lit in its own right, or to be combined with others to make an overall picture with no hard lines. These units within the set were the front room, the kitchen, the garden, the path, and the foreground.

The creation of the nuclear explosion itself presented the greatest challenge of all. This was to be far more than a simple "off-stage" noise. It was actually to be seen on stage. The target area was assumed to be some distance away and the bungalow several miles from the actual center of the blast. Therefore a few quite different effects would need to be created. These were as follows.

1 A blinding white flash

2 A shock or pressure wave (accompanied by sound effects and the semi-destruction of the bungalow on stage)

3 Heat blast and wind

4 Revelation of the aftermath

To try and create a "visible" nuclear explosion on stage, even the effect away from the epicenter, was a new and very exciting undertaking for all those concerned.

In the event, the elements actually used were all readily available. Nothing brand-new or previously unknown was made or invented. Nevertheless, the scene required a good many hours of work to fit the various effects together and to time their co-ordination correctly. (This applied particularly to the lasers.) Only then would the illusion work.

The two fundamental elements the lighting department had to deal with were the blinding flash and the heat haze. Also, after the explosion, the lighting had then to reveal the sudden desecration of the home.

First of all, the problem of how to create the nuclear flash was discussed. The director, David Neilson, wanted the flash effect to light the stage with such brilliance that the audience would be momentarily blinded. To achieve this with reflected light would be incredibly difficult. All the pre-production experiments with 5 kilowatt and 10 kilowatt luminaires proved this to be true. However, turning the lamps to face the audience did not really work either, because the filaments required such a long time to cool down.

At last, after much discussion and experimenting with various effects, a final decision was reached. The light source would have the greatest impact if it faced the audience. So the filament problem would simply have to be overcome by some means. Lighting units were therefore required which could heat up and cool down extremely quickly, rather like a strobe. The unit eventually chosen was a Jupiter Six. Each unit contained six Pars.(These were FCX : 120 volt, 650 watt.) Their quick response was just as required and the blinding effect suitably dramatic.

When the Wind Blows

The set before the nuclear explosion

The heat haze was the second special effect required. It was hoped that this would be a fairly long and progressive effect, lasting for about twenty-five seconds. We had already decided that the white flash should be directed towards the audience, so it was thought that the heat haze should also be pointed in their direction. Somehow we needed to create a swirling wave of heat which would spread above the audience. After considering all the possibilities, it seemed that using a laser was probably the only answer. This decision immediately created two more fresh problems:

In the first place, the cost, and second, how to satisfy the health and safety department that any danger had been eliminated. As it happened, both problems were quite easily overcome. This was because we elected to use four low-cost, 0.5 milliwatt neon lasers, which were no bigger than a kitchen-roll tube. They did not scan mechanically, so no special operator would be required. Moreover, these lasers were low enough in power to be considered within a category where safety regulations were readily accomodated. The units

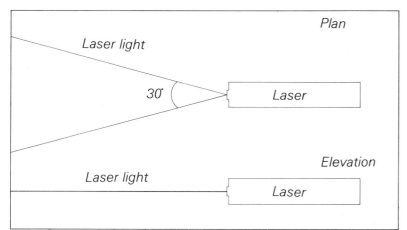

Each laser gun produced an effective "fan" of laser light

scanned optically (by beaming the laser through a lens at the end of the laser gun) to create a 30 degree "fan" of laser light.

Because neon lasers were being used, the color of the light was red — perfect for our needs! To see laser beams (or any light beam), a medium is required. After all, fresh air does not "light up". It is only the dust particles present in the air which catch and reflect the light so as to make the beam visible to our eyes. Smoke was therefore introduced to enhance the effect. It is in the nature of smoke to swirl and drift in laser light so this gave a very good impression of fierce heat. The placing of the lasers was crucial. To achieve the very best effect, the light should be aimed towards the audience, rather than coming in from behind them. The lasers would also need to be placed as low as possible, so that the audience could actually look along the length of the beam towards the laser gun. To achieve this ideal position, the laser guns would have to be placed on the stage (hopefully the direction in which the audience would be looking!)

Because of their small size, it was no problem to hide the laser guns discreetly. All that remained was to ensure that, should they drop on their axis, there could be a means of cutting off the lasers' light before it reached audience eye height. To meet this stipulation, a very simple box construction around the gun was required.

Further to this, it may be worth mentioning that lasers can, of course, create some stunning effects, and that really there is nothing that can simulate their rather special characteristics. Used sensibly and with care, they are perfectly safe.

High-powered lasers, because ◇ they are potentially dangerous if incorrectly handled, can be used only with the assistance of an experienced operator. Current health and safety regulations ensure this. There are, however, categories of laser that anyone can buy or use, provided that certain guidelines are adhered to carefully. A copy of the code of practice regarding laser use is available from any local Health and Safety department (or the Food and Drug Administration in the USA).

One slight disadvantage of using lasers is that they can only be switched on or off; so the effect may look rather abrupt. In order to avoid this unnaturally sudden appearance, it was decided to try and find a way of somehow "introducing" the lasers. To this end, a red "light curtain" was placed across the top of the proscenium arch from which the lasers' light would appear.

A light curtain is a straight row of lights, usually Pars, each of which gives as parallel a beam as can be contrived! The overall effect is a strong curtain of light. The greater the inclination of the lights' angle to the audience, the greater the effect of the curtain. A good light curtain will "mask" anything behind it, providing that the area behind remains unlit.

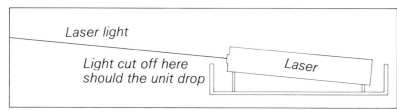

Box construction around the laser gun

When the Wind Blows

To give the right effect, the light curtain could, of course, be gradually brought up to full intensity. Once again smoke was required. This time it was used to obtain the best effect from the light curtain. Once lit, the laser light emerged from behind this curtain of light.

The wind effect was created by four wind machines, which were placed behind the proscenium and then masked by the light curtain as they were flown into position.

As the dust and debris cleared, the set was to be slowly revealed, starting first with a silhouette of the house, and then showing the broken telegraph pole and the tree now stripped of its leaves. This was achieved simply, by lighting the cyclorama and nothing else.

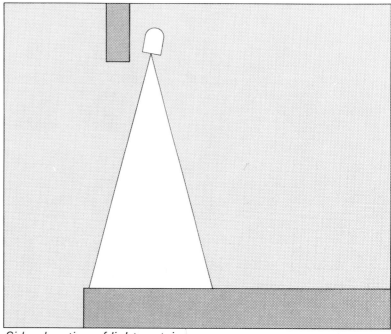

Side elevation of light curtain

The sequence of events:

Black-out
Blinding light
Sound effect: house shakes and is then devastated:
Smoke on
Light curtain on
Lasers on
Wind machines on
Wind machines off
Lasers off
Light curtain fades out
Silhouette
Complete lighting state

It may be of interest to know that the sound was not used merely to create an audible effect, but also had a dramatic physical effect. Such was the force of the sound effect, that the chandeliers, and the theater itself, literally shook. Everybody there experienced a thumping sensation on the chest.

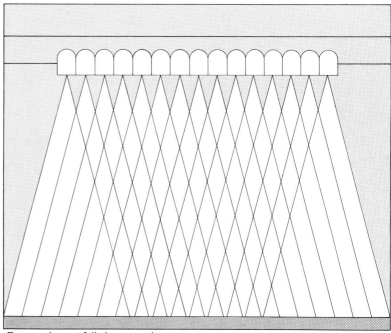

Front view of light curtain

The impression of the set being destroyed on stage, despite its not being actually visible, was convincing because of all the crashing and banging, and because of the swirling heat haze that dominated everything and looked very eerie. Most of the destruction of the set was accomplished by using electro-mechanical means.

The lighting of the set was based on very strict area separation, so that it was all easily controlled. The overall effect was of a shock to all the senses, which none of the audience would care to repeat in real life.

This combination of especially dramatic effects was made possible only by the co-operation of all the different production departments. As often happens, their particular areas of responsibility tended to overlap each other. In this instance, the mix of effects occupied just a few moments of stage time and so the impact was especially powerful.

The aftermath of the nuclear explosion

Lighting plan

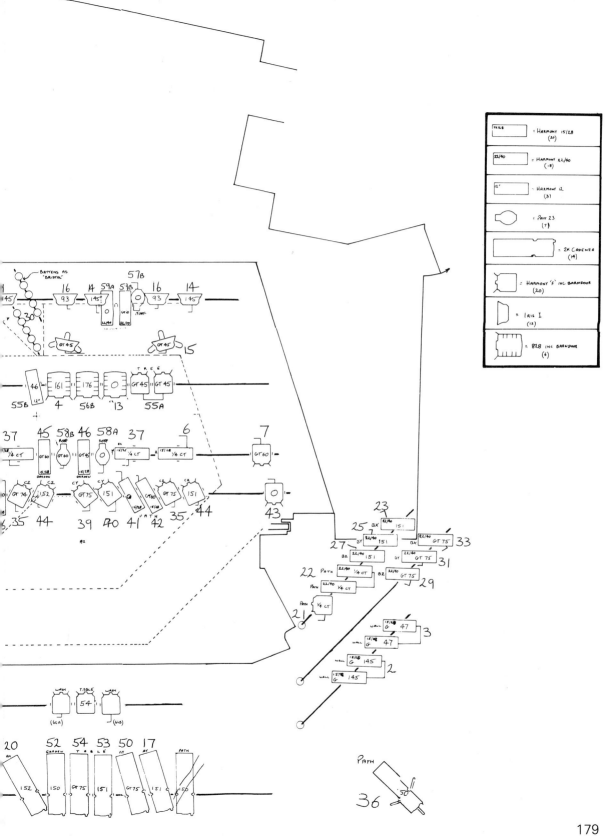

Lighting a musical

When lighting a musical, the principles remain the same as for any other production. There is no need to have sleepless nights worrying about the complexity of the lighting. It is true that there may be many more lighting states and cues than are normally required but, with careful pre-planning, this need not be such a daunting prospect. In fact it is a good opportunity for the lighting designer to explore new avenues, to enjoy the excuse to use color more lavishly than usual, and also to experiment with a few special effects.

However, the fact that the production is a musical does not imply that the work can be undertaken without discipline. Far more is involved than simply rigging lots of colored lights and using a few follow spots. Once again, every luminaire will be pre-planned and must be given a specific job to do. Follow spots, in particular, may require extra rehearsal time, so as to establish and practise cues.

Oh What a Lovely War! is an interesting production to study, not only because it is a musical, but also as the staging at the Bristol Old Vic involved a square rig, and so was rather unusual.

The set used was, in fact, very simple. It consisted of just a scaffold cube with two scaffold towers at either side. On each corner of the cube were battens of red, white, and blue bulbs that "chased" (flashed off and on in sequence). The sides, front, and back of the cube were used to hang luminaires, thus creating a square rig.

This square rig was by no means purely decorative. The front bar was used to frontlight the upstage area, the side bars to give a wash of side light, and the back bar was rigged for back light. Black masking flats were placed down the sides of the stage, thus allowing booms to be hidden behind them. On to these booms were rigged luminaires for side light and low cross light. The rest of the rig was constructed as shown on the plan at the end of this section (see pages 184-85).

It is important when lighting a musical to remember that some moments in the show may be played "straight". That is to say, there will be no music, no brash color, and no follow spots. So it is always advisable to provide a good area cover, as previously described. The stage area used in this production was such that a division of twelve sections was needed (three across and four up). This was then all marked up and lit in the normal way — except for the D area, which was used so little that only two luminaires were used for each area (one in a warm color and one in a cool).

DX	DY	DZ
CX	CY	CZ
BX	BY	BZ
AX	AY	AZ

The stage area for this production was divided into these twelve sections

Oh What a Lovely War !

The colors chosen for these front lights were normal tints (S1 Gold tint and 40 Pale blue). The same colors were used in both sides of the rig. The sculpting quality was achieved by the level difference — which meant no pairing of these luminaires was necessary. The whole area was backlit in open white for "normal" conditions.

When lighting a musical, it is a good idea to have a few really strong colored washes ready, in case there is a suitable moment in which to use them. A backlight structure is best used to avoid lighting the actors' faces with strong color. The colors for *Oh What a Lovely War!* were green, blue, and red (38, 63/20, 64).

There were certain moments in the show when the director required splashes of color, rather than a heavy wash. This was achieved by a spot bar of pattern 23's (500 watt profiles) fitted with break-up gobos. Each profile was given a different color and focused to cover all the staging area.

Under normal conditions, the image from 500 watt profiles (fitted with gobos and with moderately heavy color) would be "washed out" by the main rig lighting the actors. However, as follow spots were being used to light the actors and singers during these moments, the problem did not apply. It should be noted that quite subtle effects can be achieved by using follow spots to light actors or singers. This is sometimes a welcome relief from the powerful and bright, or highly colored lighting states so often associated with musicals.

Musicals usually contain a good deal of dance. The most flattering way of lighting body form is from the side. To shape and sculpture the dancer is often more important than highlighting the eyes and faces. In this way "lighting the dancers so they can be seen" needs a different approach. Use a good strong side light for the dance sequences and do not flatten it by adding too much front light.

Indeed, when lighting the scene at the plotting session, build the state by introducing the side light first, adding as little front light as possible if needed.

In the case of *Oh What a Lovely War!*, the side light came from three booms and one perch on each side. Further side light came from the upstage and downstage bars on stage. Their purpose was to sidelight the "normal" scenes in the play.

A five-color wash was used from the side; one straw, two blues, one pink and one white. These were set low on the boom. The first luminaire was only about half a meter from the stage floor. (Lights that are rigged this low are sometimes referred to as "shin-busters"!)

The decision to use profiles on the bottom two luminaires was taken in order that these could be shuttered off the stage floor. Because they were so low, the resulting booms would go from one side of the stage to the other, lighting just the dancers and singers without lighting the floor. This meant that gobo patterning could be used on the stage floor without being washed out by any of the stage illumination.

As can be seen from the plan at the end of this section, quite a number of specials were needed in order to light specific moments in the show.

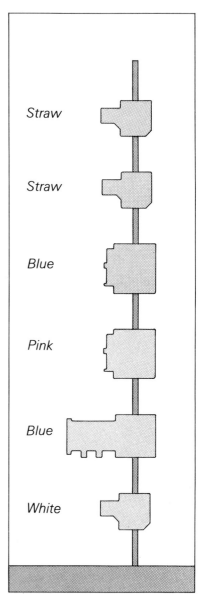

Straw

Straw

Blue

Pink

Blue

White

Typical construction of a boom used in the show, with general color description

Slide projection was also used effectively in the show. The screen was dropped in and out of position as it was required. Because the screen was not a permanent fixture, no back projection was possible. Back projection is usually preferred, as a brighter image can be achieved with this than with front projection. Moreover, with multi-slide projection, there is always a possibility of a slide becoming jammed. If the projector is on stage, it may be possible for the stage manager or a stage electrician to be able to free it. However, if the projector is in a remote position in the front of house area, then a jammed slide could spell disaster. So, when there is a choice, do elect for back projection if possible.

The careful cueing of a musical is absolutely vital if the lighting designer is to achieve a creative interpretation of the show. Very often the light cues are linked to a change of rhythm, a certain beat, or a specific dance move.

It is certainly a time when it is essential to work very closely with the stage manager or whoever will be "on the book" (cueing the show). Certainly one should spend rather more time in rehearsals than one would for a conventional play.

Taping the musical numbers can be very useful. Usually everything happens so quickly in a musical that it is impossible to take notes and watch the stage at the same time. Taping the show enables the lighting designer to plan the cues and changes in a more relaxed and efficient way.

Thus it can be seen that lighting a musical requires the same basic techniques as any other production. The role and aims of the lighting designer should remain unchanged.

In order to achieve these aims, however, the actual choice of lighting structures may differ. More side light, especially, may be used than is normal in a conventional play; as well as top or back light. Bolder, more lavish color effects may also be appropriate.

There is also the possibility of experimenting with more unusual special effects to add to the visual impact of a dance or song. Throughout, methodical pre-planning of all the cues and lighting states will be essential.

183

Lighting plan

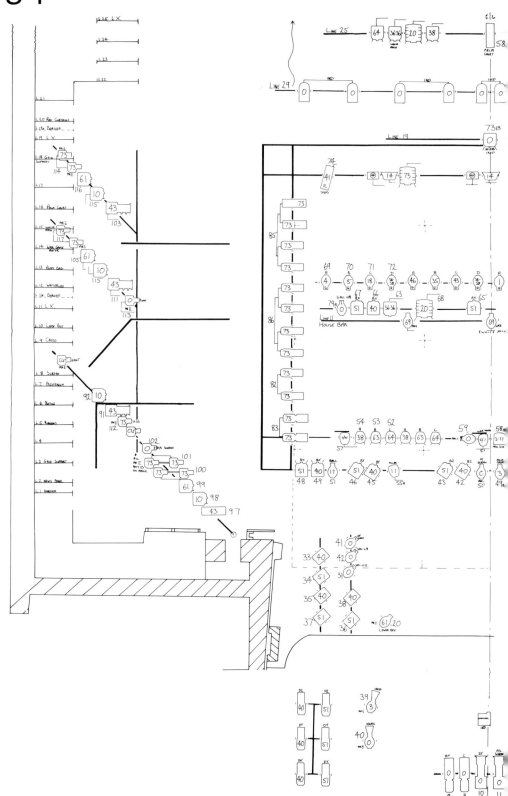

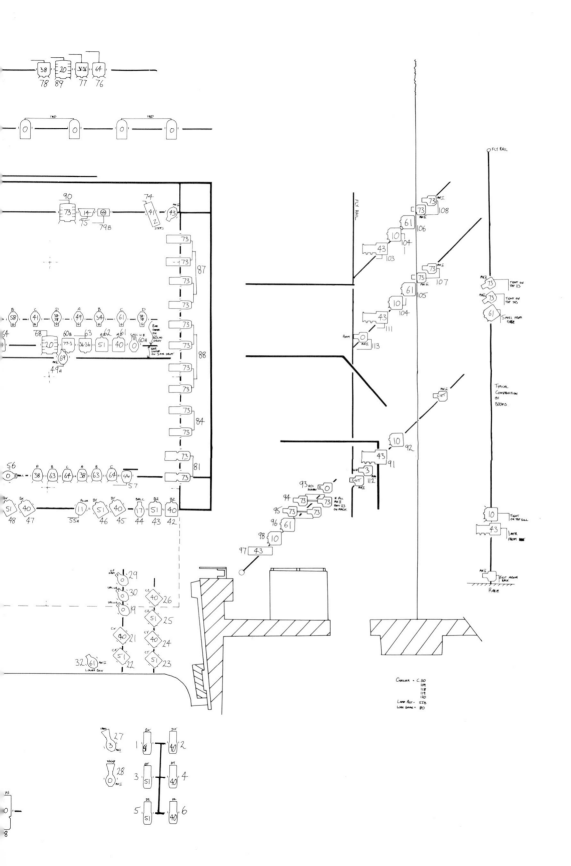

Glossary

Acting area The area of the stage upon which the actors will perform; area separation

Adapter or splitter A means by which two or more electrical devices can be made to share the same power point

Ampere A measurement of the rate of flow, or current, of an electrical circuit

Area separation Dividing the acting area of the stage into suitable units that can be lit independently or together

Auditorium The audience area beyond the stage

Backcloth A scenic canvas or "drop" used across the back of the stage, often serving as a sky-cloth

Bar Pipe or barrel above the stage for the suspension of lighting and scenery; may be called a batten

Barn doors Four separately hinged doors on a pivoted frame at the front of Fresnels or P C's. These can be used to shape the beam and prevent spill light

Batten Bar from which lighting equipment can hang: also applied to compartment-type lighting or border-lights

Blanket color Overall wash of unrelieved color of exactly the same tint

Boom or light tree A vertical pipe which can support several luminaires on a number of boom arms

Bosun's (or boatswain's) chair A wooden seat slung on a rope which is used when working aloft

Chasing lights Lights that flash on and off quickly in succession

Cinemoid Cellulose acetate which is used to make color filters in the UK

Color correction A means by which colors can be adjusted to give the desired effect; for instance, special filters may be needed to achieve a more acceptable white

Color magazine A color boomerang, a device which holds color media and enables quick changes to be made to the color of a follow spot etc.

Composite gel Different colored pieces of color gel cut to fit together into one color frame

Counterweight system Method by which apparatus can be loaded on to a flying bar and be safely balanced by weights in a cradle

Cross-fade To fade or change from one lighting state to another

Cross plugging A system whereby several luminaires can be made to share the same circuit or dimmer alternately or at different times

Cue When appertaining to lighting, this indicates the moment at which a lighting change will be initiated. The cue may be a line in the play, a change of tempo in a song, or a particular piece of action on stage — whatever has been entered on the cue sheet

Cue count The time it will take, in seconds, to execute a lighting cue

Cue sheet A chart on which all the lighting cues of a production are recorded and which the board operator or electrician will use

Cyclorama or sky-cloth A curved or straight backcloth hung at the rear of the stage. It is sometimes painted white and then lit as required

Derig The removal of the lighting rig at the end of a production

Dimmer A device which regulates the power in the circuit feeding a lamp, so as to alter the intensity of the light

Diorama A scenic view or representation made with a partly translucent painting. If the light shining through it is varied, then the effects change

Dry ice Frozen carbon dioxide which can be used to produce mist or steam effects

Earthing Means by which, for safety reasons, metal parts of electrical equipment may be wired to the ground

Fill light Light which fills the shadows the key light creates

Fit-up The rigging of the lighting equipment prior to a production

Flare Usually refers to lighting spill, or can be spectral-flare rainbow effects

Flat or peak field The distribution of light intensity

(across a beam), which can be evenly spread or concentrated in one area (peak field)

Flies The area above the stage where scenery and lighting equipment can be suspended out of sight or "flown"

Floats or footlights A batten of lights set at the front of the stage, which in historical times consisted of floating oil-wicks

Floods Floodlights giving a wide beam of light, sometimes ellipsoidal reflectors

Focusing In theatrical terminology, this does not necessarily mean achieving a sharp focus. Instead it describes organization of the direction, position, shape, and cover of the beam — as directed on the lighting plan by the lighting designer

Front of house (FOH) Lighting positioned in the auditorium which is directed towards the stage

Gate Aperture between the light source and the lens on a profile spotlight; may have built-in shutters with which the beam can be shaped, as well as runners which allow for the insertion of an iris or gobo

Gauze or scrim Large-weave cloth used for scenic effects which can be rendered either transparent or opaque according to the direction and intensity of the lighting

Gelatine A color filter medium, which is made of animal gelatin; it is rarely used nowadays

Gobo (or cookie) Template of thin metal with cutout design or pattern which can be projected; normally used with profile spotlights

Ground plan Scale drawing of a set as seen from above

Ground-row lighting Strip light lighting scenery from below; lengths of shallow lighting equipment or battens, for low-level lighting effects

Hire company A rental company

House bar A permanent flying line

Irises These can be inserted into profile spotlights to vary the size of the beam

Key light A light of high intensity, or the most dominant direction of light; the most important light on a set which focuses attention, such as moonlight through a window

Lamps The high-power electric light bulbs used in theatrical lighting equipment

Legs Unframed scenery, canvas wings, or curtains which are hung vertically to mask the sides of the stage

Lighting bar Lighting or electrics batten, or pipe

Lighting plan or plot A scale drawing detailing the exact location of each luminaire used in a production and any other pertinent information

Lighting rehearsal A rehearsal of the lighting effects on stage, usually without any

actors, during which any necessary adjustments can be made to the luminaires

Lighting state The format of lighting used at a particular time; a "lighting picture"

Lighting structures The different angles of light used in stage lighting: top light, side light, front light etc.

Light tree See Boom

Luminaire tails Electrical pigtails or lantern tail; the ends of cable attached to a luminaire

Luminaires The instruments, lanterns, or units used to light the stage; lighting fixtures

Magazine battens Border lights or battens which are "flown" above the stage (UK)

Mains operated British term meaning electrically powered, using the "mains" voltage at local or domestic level

Masking To hide certain parts of the stage or equipment from the audience, using scenic devices

Masque A popular court entertainment in 16th and 17th century Europe, performed by masked players and usually based on a mythological theme. It often included music, dance, and poetry, as well as spectacular effects

Master A dimmer control (a fader) which controls other submasters, which in turn control the dimmers

Mock-up A structural model of the stage and set, often a

Glossary

forerunner to the final detailed model, made to scale

Open (or exposed) rig A rig used on an open, unmasked stage without a proscenium arch or borders, so the lighting will be visible and not hidden from the audience in the conventional way

Pairing lamps Joining more than one luminaire to one circuit

Panoramas A painted cloth which can be wound across the stage to reveal a constantly changing view

Patching Using a cross-connect panel which allows any of the stage circuits to use any of the dimmers

Perches Platforms set behind the proscenium arch and used for lighting equipment; luminaires positioned in this area are sometimes called tormentor spots

"Practical" A lighting fixture which is apparently used on the set by the actors during the production, and so is visible to the audience and must be operational. Can also mean any fixture or prop which is illuminated

Preset A group of faders. Can also mean a pre-arranged lighting state being held in readiness for future use

Profile spot Ellipsoidal reflector spotlight; provides a soft or hard-edged beam of light focused by a lens system

Proscenium arch The stage opening which, in a traditional theater, separates the actors

from the audience: sometimes called the "fourth wall"

Pyrotechnics May mean fireworks, but in lighting circles generally refers to any bangs or flashes that might be required!

Raked stage A sloping area of stage which is raised at the back (up stage) end

Rig The lighting construction or arrangement of equipment for a particular production

Roundel Can mean a colored glass filter used on striplights. In the historical section of this book, it refers to a small circular window or niche

Run-through or run Seeing a performance of a play (or one aspect of it, such as the lighting) all the way through, from beginning to end

SCR Abbreviation for a silicon-controlled rectifier; a solid state semi-conductor device which operates as a high-speed switch and is used in dimmers

Shutters Part of a luminaire which determines the profile of the beam and can be used to prevent lighting spill on the edges of the stage or set

Sightlines Imaginary lines drawn from the eyes of the audience to the stage, to determine the limits of stage which will be visible from the auditorium

Specials Any light which is used for a special purpose or isolated moment in a production rather than being used for general area lighting

Spill light Unwanted light which spills over its required margins or shows through a gap

Spot bar Batten or pipe on which spotlights are hung

Stage cloth or drop A vertical area of painted canvas which can be a backcloth, front cloth, or drop cloth, depending on its position on the stage

Submaster This controls a number of faders in a group master control system, and is in turn controlled by the master dimmer on the consul

Tabs Stage curtains across proscenium arch

Tallescope A scaffolding, mobile tower which enables electricians to rig the luminaires at a height of up to thirty-six feet

Temperature The warmth or coolness of lighting colors

Throw distance Distance between a luminaire and the area on the stage that it will light

Thrust stage A stage which is surrounded by the audience on three sides

Tormentors Masking flats angled up stage and set at the edge of the proscenium

Tripe (bundle) Bunch of cables bound into single strand

Tripe ends or pigtail Short cable that protrudes from a connecting strip or drop box (US) at the end of a stage circuit

Volt A unit measurement of electrical pressure between two points in a single circuit

Index

A

Acting area 55, 76, 96, 102
cover 89, 96 , 146
dividing the, 76
Adapters
(splitters) 92
Alternating current 36, 152
Angelo, Henry 15
Appia, Adolphe 17-18
Auditorium 13, 14, 17, 42, 59, 98
Avoiding shadows 44, 58,96
Awkward areas 67

B

Backcloths 14, 17, 18
Back light 22, 32, 46,84, 85, 103, 121, 146 , 182
Barn doors 30, 31, 94, 147
Battens 13, 15, 18, 33, 59, 103,121, 180
Beam *see* Light beam
Beam projector 28
Bean-can luminaires 57,149
The Bengal Lancer 109
Black-out 36, 58, 64
Board operator 40-1, 61, 97, 98-9
Bomb tank 126
Booms 13, 69, 96, 160
Bottom light *see* Up light
Bouncing bars 24
Brecht 19

C

Cables 42, 92, 94-5, 96, 154
Calculating current 155
Candlelight 13, 14
Candles 13, 14, 131
Carbon arc 16-18
Ceilings 68
Chandelier 13, 14

Cinemoid 105
Circuit breakers 155, 157
Circuits 97, 98,148, 152
electrical 150, 152
Clouds 17, 118-9
Color 15, 17, 60, 89, 92, 100-11, 149, 161, 180
choosing 60,100, 105, 168-9
coding 34
correction 104, 144
filters 60, 92, 102, 103, 104- 5
frame holders 28
mixing 102
washes 82, 144, 146, 182
wheel 105, 145, 146, 162
Colored water 12
Comedie Française, 16
Composite colors 104
Composite gobos 123
Computer control 19, 40- 1, 98
Control boards 37-41, 42, 61, 98, 99, 144
Controlling electrical energy 152
Counterweights 94
Covent Garden 16
Craig, Edward G. 18
Creating a galaxy 114
Cross light 160-1
see *also* Side light
Cross plugging 148
Crystal sphere 12, 19
Cue 61, 180, 183
number 98
sheet 65-6
synopsis 98
Curtains 61
Cyclorama 17, 19, 33, 49, 50, 54, 55, 70, 115, 116, 118, 161
tenting the, 70, 160-1

D

Dance or ballet 45, 182
Darkening the stage 14, 16
see also Black-out
Davy, Sir Humphry 16

"Dead" areas 147
De Loutherbourg, Philip 15
Dimmers 19, 36, 40, 42, 146, 147
setting up 36
Dioramas 15, 16
Disc effects 118-20
Discussion stage 67, 74
Di Soni, Leone 12
Down light 32, 47
see also Top light
Dress rehearsal 90, 99
Drummond, Thomas 16
Dry ice 22, 128

E

Earthing 153, 157
Electrical check 34, 94
Electrical team
see Lighting crew
Electrician 40-1, 97, 98'
Electricity 17, 36, 150-7
Epitaxial lamp 32

F

Fader 36-7
Fill light 44, 45, 83, 84
Fire effects 129
Fire regulations 57
First rehearsal 74
Fishtail burner 16
Fit-up *see* Rig
Flare 30
Flash box 127
Flash powder 127
Flat field 29
Floats *see* Footlights
Flood, the 33, 54
Fluorescent paint 60
Focusing 96
Pars 32
profiles 29
the Fresnel 30
session 24, 90, 93, 95-6
team 96-7
Follow spot 58, 61,180,182

Index

Footlights 13, 14, 15, 17, 48, 54
Fountains 16, 124
Fresnel spot 30, 54, 84, 97, 147
Front light 44, 46, 61, 81, 85, 87, 145, 146
Fuses 153-4, 155, 157
pyrotechnic, 127

G

Garrick, David 15
Gas lighting 16, 17
Gate 28, 30
Gauze 15, 17, 22, 59, 118, 121, 161
transformations 121
Gels 104-5, 116
German influence, 18
Gobos 29, 54, 60-1, 104, 120, 122-3, 169
creating moving images 124
making, 60. 123,
using mesh in, 118, 124
The Gondoliers 110-111
Ground *see* Earthing
Ground plan, the 72
see also Lighting plan
Ground rows 33, 49

H

Herkomer 17, 18
Hiring equipment 54, 92,
History of lighting 10-19
125, 127
Home-made luminaires
57, 149

I

Ingegneri, Angelo 12
Insurance 54
Iris 29, 58, 122
Irving, Sir Henry 16-17
Italian influence 12

J

Jablochkov Candle 16
Jones, Inigo 12, 15

K

Key light 32, 44, 45, 83, 84, 98
Kipling 107
Koltain, Ralph 19
Komisarjevsky 19

L

Ladder 57, 93, 94, 96, 97
crew 97
Lamps 13, 33, 35, 92, 116, 145, 149, 156
bases 35
changing 35
colored 116
Lasers 50, 60, 174-5
Lenses 29, 30-1, 125, 132, 141
Light
beams 29, 30-1, 54, 86
boxes 116-7
curtain 121, 175-6
levels 98, 99, 146-7
trees *see* Booms
Lighting
bars 94-5
crew 24, 92-3, 94, 96-7
design 22, 74- 5
designer 13-19, 20-5, 62, 97
desk 37, 40-1
plan 72, 76, 85, 86, 92, 95
plot 98
rehearsal 97-8
see also Lighting session
session 86, 98
spill 17, 59, 97
stand 57
structures 44-50, 72, 76, 87-9
symbols 72-3
Lightning 12, 120
Limelight 16
Luminaires 19, 28-34, 54,

95-6, 96-7, 123, 147, 155
maintenance 34
mark up 86
see also
Flood, the
Follow spot
Fresnel spot
Pars
Pebble convex
luminaire
Profile spot
Spotlights

M

Machinery 14, 15
Mains electrical supply 152
Management 24
Manual lighting boards 37-9, 99
Maroons 126
Masking 13, 17, 22, 59, 68, 160
Masks, negative and positive 118-9
The Masque of Blackness 13
Masques 13, 14
Masters 37
Mechanical check 34
Memory control systems 40-1, 98
A Midsummer Night's Dream 160-65
Mirrors 61, 67
Model of the set 67, 71, 74, 141
Moons 12, 115, 118-9
Moving water 120
Musical 19, 102
Lighting a, 180-85

N

Neon signs 116-7
Night effects 60, 114-15, 118-9, 160

O

Oh What a Lovely War! 180-5
Oil lamps 13-15
electrically operated 130
mains operated 130
battery operated 130-1
radio controlled 131
Oil lighting 13, 15, 16, 48
Operator *see* Electrician
Optical check 34

P

Pairing lamps 42, 89, 92, 147, 148
Panoramas 15
Parallel wiring 156
Pars 32, 84, 121, 173, 175
Patching 42-3
Patch panel 42-3,
Peak field 29
Pebble-convex luminaire 31
Pepys, Samuel 14
Peter Pan 108
Phase control 36
Plugs 34, 42-3, 95, 96
Practicals 61, 64, 96
Pre-planning 62, 92
Presets 37
Primary colors 102
Production procedure 90-99
Production team 22, 67, 74, 90, 98
Profile spot 19, 28, 54, 84, 120, 122
Projecting images 122
Projectors and projection 17, 18, 31, 60, 67, 114, 115, 118-9, 120, 122-3, 124-5, 132-141, 162, 183
Pyrotechnics 22, 126-7
Pyrotechnic fuses 127

R

Rain effects 120

The Recruiting Officer 166-171
Reinhardt, 18
Renaissance, the 12, 15
Reproducing lighting structures on paper 72
Resistance 150, 152
Ridge, Harold 19
Rig 24, 155,
constructing the, 24, 92-3, 95-6
open 67
planning the, 74
removing the, 90, 92, 94
square 180-1
Ring Round the Moon 107
Ripple machines 120

S

Sabbattini 13
Sacrificial gel 105
Safety 56-7, 92, 94, 121, 126, 150-7
chains 56, 96
Samoiloff 19
San Gallo 12
Scamozzi 12
Scrim *see* Gauze
SCRs 36
Script analysis 22, 64-66
Series wiring 156
Serlio, Sebastiano 12
Short, Harold 19
Shutters 29, 34
Side light 45, 69, 85, 87, 182
Silhouette 50, 88, 118
Sky-cloth 49, 118, 166,
Slide distortion 132-9
Smoke 13, 50, 61, 121, 126, 128, 162, 175, 176
gun 128
screen 50-1
Snow 120
bag 120
Special effects 22, 60, 112-131
Specials 61, 84, 148
Spot bars 59, 95, 96

Spotlights 16, 17, 28-30, 45
Stage
cloth 20
labeling the, 77-80
lighting the, 81-2
sections 76-82, 84
Stars 114
Stencils 72-3
Stepped lens 30
Strobes 120, 121
Sun box 116

T

Tallescopes 24, 95
Technical rehearsal 98-9
Template 134 *see* Gobo
Texturing and "break-up" patterns 122, 169, 182
Theater in the round 88-9, 166-9
Thrust stage 87
Top light 47, 89
Transformation powder 127
Transformers 157
Triacs 36

U

Up light 48, 162

W

Water effects 120
Waveforms 36, 152-3
Wavelength 102
When the Wind Blows 108, 172-79
Windows 12, 29, 83-4
stained glass 123

Bibliography and Acknowledgements

Bellman, Willard F.
Lighting the Stage; Art and Practice
Crowell 1974

Bentham, Frederick
Art of Stage Lighting
Pitman House Ltd 1980

Bergman, Gosta M.
Lighting in the Theater
Rowman and Littlefield 1977

Gillette, J. Michael
Designing with Light
Mayfield Publishing Company 1978

Hughs, G.J.
Electricity and Buildings
Peregrinus 1984

McCandless, Stanley
A Method of Lighting the Stage
Theater Arts Books 1958

McPartland, J.F.
Handbook of Practical Electrical Design
McGraw-Hill 1984

Morris, Noel M.
Electrical Circuits and Systems
Macmillan 1980

It is also important to read the **National Electric Code (USA) And the IEE Regulations (UK)**

Palmer, Richard H.
The Lighting Art: The Aesthetics of Stage Lighting Design
Prentice-Hall Inc. 1985

Parker, W. Oren & Smith, Harvey K.
Scene Design and Stage Lighting
Holt, Rinehart & Winston Inc. 1979

Pilbrow, Richard
Stage Lighting
Cassell Ltd 1979

Reid, Francis
Stage Lighting Handbook
Pitman 1982
A & C Black 1982

Rosenthal, Jean & Wertenbaeker, Lael
The Magic of Light
Little Brown & Co. 1972

Sellman, Hunton D. & Lessley, Merrill
Essentials of Stage Lighting
Prentice-Hall Inc. 1982

Thompson, Francis G.
Electrical Installation and Workshop Technology
Longman 1984

Warfel, William B.
Handbook of Stage Lighting Graphics
Drama Book Specialists Publishers 1974

Rank Strand Limited
PO Box 51, Great West Road,
Brentford, Middlesex, TW8 9HR
United Kingdom
CCT Theatre Lighting Limited
Windsor House, 26 Willow Lane,
Mitcham, Surrey, CR4 4NA United Kingdom
**Theatre Projects Covent
Garden Limited**
10-16 Mercer Street, London, WC2H 9QE
United Kingdom
Meltdown Limited
57-59 Long Acre, London, WC2E 9JZ
United Kingdom

Raymond Biggs
Illustrator and author of *When the Wind Blows*
and the publishers:
Hamish Hamilton
Garden House 57-59 Long Acre, London.
WC2E 9JZ   United Kingdom
Bristol Old Vic Trust Limited
Theatre Royal, King Street, Bristol, BS1 4ED
United Kingdom
Mike and Tim Evans (Small beginnings)
John Elvery (Notes on projection)
G. John Davies B.Sc., C.Eng.,MIEE
(Consultant engineer)